In Search of
GOD'S
MAN

A HELP FOR PULPIT COMMITTEES

Foreword by Bob Jones III

Douglas E. DeVore

BJU PRESS
GREENVILLE, SOUTH CAROLINA

Library of Congress Cataloging-in-Publication Data

DeVore, Douglas E., 1946
    In search of God's man / Douglas E. DeVore ; foreword by Bob Jones III
    p. cm.
    ISBN 1-57924-819-5 (perfect bound pbk. : alk. paper)
    1. Clergy—Appointment, call, and election. I. Title
    BV664 .D48 2002
    254—dc21
                                                2202002571

The format and contents of the forms in the Appendices of this book may be used without permission.

The fact that materials produced by other publishers may be referred to in this volume does not constitute an endorsement by Bob Jones University Press of the content or theological position of materials produced by such publishers. The position of Bob Jones University Press, and of the University itself, is well known. Any references and ancillary materials are listed as an aid to the reader and in an attempt to maintain the accepted academic standards of the publishing industry.

Cover image by TJ Getz

All Scripture is quoted from the Authorized King James Version.

In Search of God's Man
Douglas E. DeVore

Design by TJ Getz
Composition by Milthon Martínez-Jiménez

©2002 by Bob Jones University Press
Greenville, South Carolina 29614

Printed in the United States of America
All rights reserved

ISBN 1-57924-819-5

15 14 13 12 11 10 9 8 7 6 5 4 3 2 1

CONTENTS

FOREWORD

When Doug DeVore asked me if the BJU Press would be interested in publishing a book he was writing to help churches searching for a new pastor, my answer was an emphatic "YES!" I had seen so many churches flounder, divide, or collapse for lack of understanding about how to proceed from "old" to "new." I doubt that there is any time in a church's life that leaves so much potential for satanic disruption than that church's "wilderness wandering" without a Moses. Their pastor has left, and the "Aarons" who remain were never given direction and instruction for their responsibilities to the people of God in the wilderness.

Doug DeVore and his committee found themselves in this predicament on more than one occasion. The discomfort he experienced has produced compassion for others in similar circumstances. *In Search of God's Man* is the outflow of God-granted and experience-taught wisdom.

Truthfully, this is two books in one. The practical material in the appendix is worth the price of the book itself. I cannot imagine a single thing the church needs to know about finding a new pastor that Doug has not provided.

Proverbs 14:15 says, ". . . the prudent man looketh well to his going." Every church is going to need the help of this book. The church that does not need it today will need it tomorrow. The deacon/elder board chairman, or the pastor, needs to invest in a copy for the sake of the church's future. Sooner or later every church will begin a journey in search of a new pastor. That journey requires a road map, and that is what this book is. It would be prudent to have this "road map" on the shelf so that an orderly and wise process can take place. The agony Doug and his committee experienced can be spared others. Their pain can be others' gain.

There is no need for the pastoral search to be an ordeal of trial and error. It will always be a trial of faith, of course, because the pastoral choice is the Lord's. By faith, we seek to know His mind in the matter. By following the recommendations of this book, the likelihood of "error" is removed. This book is a gift from God to America's Bible-believing churches.

Bob Jones III

President, Bob Jones University
Greenville, South Carolina

ACKNOWLEDGMENTS

I am forever indebted to two fine and gracious pastors who always made themselves available to this man when he needed godly advice. I am a beneficiary of their words of encouragement, wisdom, and guidance. While Dr. Harry J. Love and Dr. Wayne VanGelderen have both gone on to be with their Lord, their ministries continue. I also want to express my sincere appreciation to several members of Faith Baptist Church who were instrumental in helping me develop this book.

INTRODUCTION

No one likes surprises, yet they take place. Unfortunately, change sometimes catches us unaware and unprepared. Frequently, changing the status quo produces opposition. Whether change is desired or forced upon us, it is advantageous to have a plan in place.

Has your church gone through the process of finding a pastor? If it has not, rest assured the inevitable will happen. It is not a matter of "if" but rather "when" your need to find a pastor will take place. When the time comes, your church needs to be fully equipped to handle the responsibility. The churchwide experience of finding a pastor can range from exhilarating to devastating. The outcome is determined by many factors under your initial control. Ultimately, you must learn to transfer "your control" into Spirit-led management.

A number of protestant denominations provide a superintendency that assists in finding, if not in mandating, a congregation's pastor. In contrast, independent churches are often left to their own private resources. By their very nature, independent churches believe in the autonomy of the local church. While that position is scripturally correct, a congregation will face some interesting challenges when it comes to finding God's man to fill a vacant pulpit.

This book is written to assist local church leaders find a senior pastor for their congregation. Some readers will view this text from a preparatory perspective. "What procedures can be put in place that will facilitate a smooth transition in the future?" The needs of others may be more immediate. They may be currently struggling with the process of finding a pastor. Either way, this book is meant to be practical in its approach.

The following chapters will reflect scriptural principles, personal experiences of the author as he has worked with pastoral search committees, and tried and proven techniques. Included are documents that you may find useful as your committee develops a strategy for establishing the process of the search. This text is not meant to be absolute or all-encompassing. It merely presents you with options and suggestions. May you find this information relevant and helpful as you seek the Lord's will as you are *In Search of God's Man.*

1

Is Your House in Order?

Thou wilt keep him in perfect peace, whose mind is stayed on thee:
because he trusteth in thee. Isaiah 26:3

Order and harmony by their very definition are virtually synonymous.
Being in God's will yields peace not only in the life of an individual
Christian but also in the church as well. However, aligning yourself with
Christ has made you and your church a target of attack (Ephesians 6:12).
Anywhere that defenses are compromised, discord, disagreement, conflict,
and dissent rear their ugly heads. There is a sense of urgency in Paul's imperative "stand therefore" as he expresses our obligation to be outfitted for the
battle that rages all around us (Ephesians 6:14). An effective tactic of warfare has always been to catch the enemy unaware. In every battle there are
casualties. Today pastors are vacating pulpits at alarming rates. Where is the
local church to turn?

There is no better place to begin than "in the beginning." The account
of Creation itself, found in Genesis 1, describes how God brought forth
order out of chaos. He began with a formless void (v. 2) and separated the
light from the darkness (v. 4), the sky from the waters (vv. 6-7), the sea from
the land (v. 9), and the day from the night (v. 14). Through the very breath
of God order had been introduced to a new world. One cannot read the
sixty-six books of Scripture without realizing that among the many attributes defining our God is that of our sovereign Lord being a God of order.

As Jesus Christ spoke to His disciples, our Lord substantiated not only His authority in creating the church but also a promise for preserving it as well (Matthew 16:13-20). He was, and continues to be, the very essence of the church's existence. Devotion to Christ was preeminent in the worship of early church members as they focused upon His redeeming death and the power of God unveiled when Christ was resurrected. Early Christians worshiped, witnessed, prayed, fellowshiped, and hoped for His return. Paul described the similarities between the human body and the life of the church in I Corinthians 12:12-31. Every believer, endowed by God with specific talents and gifts, was seen as vital to the function of the whole.

An organization is a collection of people, comprised of interdependent parts, formed into a body sharing a central or common purpose. There can be found patterns of influence and authority (governance from both internal and external forces). There are rules of operation that can be framed in the light of church practice and policy.

The church is the body of Christ enlivened by an ever-present Holy Spirit. In contrast, but not in conflict, the church is also an organization. The presence of that organization is seen in its mission (or vision) and its internal structure. The members will need to agree upon statements of beliefs and rules of order. Established within its constitution or membership manual will be the format for making decisions, delineation of the structures of power, guidelines for expected order, and accountability of the membership.

A church is more than a mere collection of Christians who have decided to join a local organization. There needs to be a practical application of God's holiness in order for holiness to play a key role in the values of the organization. At stake will be the very purpose for its existence. How authority exercises its role of leadership and how the membership carries out the sacred trust of service must be shaped by His will. Faith, hope, and love were more than mere philosophical, theological platitudes to the early church. They were a way of life worth dying for. They should be no less meaningful for us today. Paul reminds us in I Corinthians 14:40 that as we carry out our commissioned responsibilities we are to "let all things be done decently and in order."

Let us now shift our thoughts into the twenty-first century. The purposes of today's church should still be

- to worship our Lord (John 4:24),
- to teach and preach God's Word (Acts 5:42),
- to seek to win the lost to Christ, locally and afar (Matthew 18:11),
- to serve and edify believers (I Thessalonians 5:11),
- and to administer the ordinances of the New Testament (I Corinthians 11:26).

These basic practices can still be found in Bible-believing and preaching churches today. The mission is still in force; what is different from the first-century church is the man-made managerial structure of the organization. Taking into account the precepts of the entire Word of God, independent churches today design their own way of managing their local church. Constitutions have been written that address issues of governance within the local body. Churches don't operate in complete isolation; they often share ideas, goals, and strategies. Good Christian colleges are giving guidance to pastors and laymen alike on the polity of the local church. So where is the problem?

Remember the old axiom "If something is working, don't fix it"? Today that mentality seems to often play itself out not only in our personal and business lives but in church administration as well. Writing or revamping a constitution can be a time-consuming task and consequently gets only a small amount of attention. Especially when things are going along quite smoothly within a church, attending to the church's constitution can be given low priority. Some readers might find it difficult to lay their hands on a personal copy of their church's constitution. If you were to walk into the church office and ask your pastor (or his secretary) for a copy of your church's constitution, you would probably see the concern on his face as he tried to figure out the motive behind your sudden request. "Surely this member is up to something," he might well be thinking. Instead of causing unease many churches go along in a "just fine thank you" mode for so many years with constitutions that have been given little to no thought. What happens should a problem arise? Will you have a manual that speaks to the issues, or will you be left holding a document that is so antiquated that it does not even reflect your current ministry?

That very scenario became reality for my church when we lost a pastor who had been there for nearly two decades. As a body of believers we were of course shaken by the news. Hope of a clearly articulated solution soon vanished as we dusted off our constitution. The church covenant and the articles of faith were clear and still relevant. How we were to address our need of finding a senior pastor left us wanting. Our constitution was dreadfully silent on what committees needed to be formed and how the membership of those committees was to be determined. Believing that our Lord is not the author of confusion, we realized that we were temporarily in that state due to our own negligence. Certainly now was not the time to launch an effort to rewrite the church's constitution. Lengthy debates would surely ensue. Any debate at this vulnerable time in our church's history could have fractured the unity we had been experiencing. The energy that should have been directed toward finding our next pastor would have been swallowed up in the process of updating our constitution. An incomplete constitution that is silent on issues leaves the leadership of the church in a tenuous position. Our dilemma could easily have escalated into a crisis. Leadership resolved this predicament by having the deacon chairman go before the congregation to openly share their plan. The congregation rallied around the deacons as they pledged to (1) abide by the constitution as much as possible, (2) press on with the task of finding a senior pastor, and (3) address the rewriting of our constitution soon after our new pastor had been installed.

As the deacons promised, after the new pastor arrived, we rewrote our constitution. It did take a significant amount of time, but time now was our ally. The amendments were adopted by the congregation without incident. We found that a simple paragraph, inserted in the "General Committees" section of our constitution, was all that it would take to set a more efficient plan in place. We believe that the following language clearly articulates our church's position:

> At the time of a vacancy for the office of senior pastor the deacon board shall become the pulpit committee. The committee shall have an internally elected chairman, vice-chairman, and secretary. (The current deacon board chairman is not eligible to hold office within the pulpit committee.) The pulpit committee shall be dissolved at the election of a new senior pastor.

It was easy for the congregation to agree with this amendment. At their last annual business meeting the congregation had already elected men that they knew were godly men as defined in I Timothy 3:8-12. These laymen had already been entrusted with the highest level of spiritual responsibility in the local church. As a result of this new language being inserted into our constitution, the deacon board now had the indisputable authority to respond immediately to a future vacancy of the senior pastor position.

In addition to the amendment found above, a more detailed segment was included in a section dedicated to the position of senior pastor. It reads as follows:

> Election. Proceedings for calling a senior pastor will officially begin by the commissioning of a pulpit committee which is the entire deacon board. This commissioning will take place in a special business meeting called for that purpose where the chairman of the pulpit committee (who shall not be the chairman of the current deacon board) shall set forth a procedure that the deacon board will follow during the calling process. This will be followed by a church-wide time of dedicatory prayer for all the efforts of the pulpit committee. (It shall be the

responsibility of the deacon board to schedule additional prayer time, encourage personal prayer and fasting, and foster an atmosphere that is conducive to spiritual growth during the interim period.)

The pulpit committee shall thoroughly investigate and prayerfully consider all candidates and make a report to the congregation at least once a month. As the Holy Spirit leads, they shall present the name of one candidate at a time for the approval by the church at a special business meeting called for that purpose. The time and purpose of this meeting must be announced beforehand in at least two regular services of the church. Before the candidate is presented to be voted on, the pulpit committee must secure his permission and present to the church, at the time of voting, a signed statement signifying the candidate's unreserved acceptance of the church's Covenant and Articles of Faith. A two-thirds majority of the voting members present shall be required to call a senior pastor. The vote shall be by secret ballot. Should the candidate fail to receive the necessary majority or refuse the call, the pulpit committee shall seek another acceptable candidate.

These two paragraphs may not be perfect nor will they suit the needs of every church represented by the readers of this text, but they meet the needs of our congregation. Consider again these key elements:

- When needed, the deacon board is empowered to exercise authority immediately.
- The pulpit committee's internal makeup is addressed.
- The scope and tenure of the committee's commission is outlined.
- A commissioning prayer service is held (1) to seek God's mind and blessing and (2) to involve every member of the church.
- There is to be regular communication between the committee and the congregation.
- The committee is to present one candidate at a time for congregational approval.
- A minimum percentage must be met before a congregational call can be extended. The secret ballot yields a more accurate picture of the congregation's wishes.

- The candidate is in concert with the church's covenant and statements of faith.

Was the experience of being caught with an outdated constitution unique to our church? No, it happens all too often. There are undoubtedly churches today that are successfully conducting business without truly functional constitutions. Their church continues with singleness of purpose due to the strong leadership of current pastor(s) and/or deacons—while not overlooking the grace of God. However, the clock is ticking.

Rules of order for a church should not be left to the most outspoken leader(s) or congregational members. The potential for disaster is obvious. A constitution needs to be written to reflect the composite beliefs of a specific congregation. The document should be under periodic review. *The best time to conduct an update is when things are going along smoothly within a church.* Preferably the constitution should be updated when there is the least opportunity for hidden agendas to be a compelling factor in deciding the means of operation. Constitutions written under duress have a tendency to be reactionary. Once beyond the fundamentals, these constitutions disclose what peculiar issues and problems the church may have recently encountered. This may result in language that is capricious and arbitrarily restrictive.

Obtain a copy of your church's constitution and review it carefully—**every word**. Your constitution is second only to the Word of God in setting the pattern for leadership within your fellowship. It is very important for the leadership of the church to abide by this document. Nothing will undermine the spirit of a church more effectively than finding out that leadership is on a self-directed course paying little to no attention to the constitution established by congregational vote. If you find that practice doesn't align itself with your rules of order, then you are faced with two choices. Either everyone abides by the constitution, or the congregation modifies the constitution to reflect the needed changes. No matter what—you must be able to abide by your constitution. Know what the document says because a crisis will reveal its true depth and value, or lack thereof.

It is time for you to ask yourself a very simple question: "IS OUR HOUSE IN ORDER?"

2

So You've Lost Your Pastor

He that dwelleth in the secret place of the most High shall abide under the shadow of the Almighty. I will say of the Lord, He is my refuge and my fortress: my God; in him will I trust. Psalm 91:1-2

The psalmist in these verses encourages himself, having repeatedly experienced the Lord's protection from danger. David knew that he served a God who thoroughly understood his every predicament. While David's attacks were against his life, the Devil's attacks against our churches today are no less real or intense. Whether your pastor has left on the very best terms or not, rest assured the Devil will try to capitalize upon the situation and threaten the well-being of your church.

Are you aware that your pastor is a gift to your congregation from God? In Ephesians 4:11 Paul states, "And **he gave** some, apostles; and some, prophets; and some, evangelists; and some, *pastors and teachers.*" The Lord gave you your pastor. Meditating upon that truth should revolutionize the way you treat and take care of him. Appreciate him for what he is—God's gift to you and to others in your local assembly. For what purpose did God give us this gift of a pastor? Paul continues, "for the perfecting of the saints, for the work of the ministry, for the edifying of the body of Christ." The pastor is called to minister the Word to his congregation. The Holy Spirit then enables and empowers the congregation to minister to others. God does not send us a pastor so that the pastor can do all of the work but rather to assist in preparing us so that we can be co-laborers for Him. Through the leadership of this under-shepherd, synergy, cohesiveness, and unity of spirit and purpose are brought to your congregation. As a result of losing your pastor, these benefits (and others) may be in jeopardy. Having no senior pastor puts the local church in a vulnerable position. The Lord in I Peter 5:8 refers to the Devil, our adversary, as a lion that "walketh about, seeking whom he may devour." The lion in this passage appears to be in no hurry. He walks and stalks his prey. He is seeking any advantage in an effort to devour whatever or whomever he can. Lions usually prey upon the most vulnerable: the sick, the weak, the slow, the lame, and the inattentive. The healthiest may not avoid his advances but they do generally avoid his deadly grasp. The church without a pastor is in possibly its most vulnerable state. Even if that vulnerable time is ever so brief, the adversary will seldom miss the opportunity to advance upon the church.

While there are unique characteristics in every situation in which a pulpit is vacated, there are similarities as well. Three circumstances that families face illustrate this point. Having lost their pastor, the emotions of a congregation may fall, at least in part, into one of these three categories: the marriage, the divorce, or the death.

The Marriage: Some of you have experienced the privilege of giving your daughter away in marriage. After prayer and much conversation with your daughter, you both have agreed that this is God's will for her life. The man to whom she is being drawn is godly and has a life desire of wanting to please God with all that he has and does. While there is a great deal of satisfaction in knowing that we should encourage this future relationship, there is also a sense of inner emptiness. The closeness created by years of careful attention by a mother and father is about to change forever. Knowing it to be God's will helps parents through this experience.

There are those times when God calls a pastor to another ministry. When a pastor knows that God is making His will abundantly clear that his current ministry is coming to a close, he will oftentimes share this news with his congregation. Over a period of time they both agree that this is God's will. The pastor may even play a key role in finding his replacement before he leaves that church. Knowing that this is

God's will leaves one in a position that he would have it no other way. While there is that quiet happiness, there is also the emptiness created by years of being together.

In these cases in which there has been open dialogue between a pastor and his congregation, the transition is fairly smooth. If a replacement has been found before the pastor vacates his position, the transition is generally even smoother. A word of caution: If a man retires from the pastorate and chooses to stay within that congregation, it may present some problems for the next pastor to effectively lead this flock. Members of the congregation may continue to seek the guidance and counsel of the retired pastor. This may happen with or without the knowledge and approval of the new senior pastor. In either case the retired pastor may unintentionally block the ability of the new pastor to shepherd his flock. The methodology and leadership style of the two men may differ. Even if the retired pastor is "assisting behind the scenes," he may inadvertently blunt the new pastor's ability to carry out his God-given responsibilities. Again, caution is advised.

The Divorce: We live in a society in which divorce happens at a most alarming rate. We often speak of the children and the abandoned spouse as "victims" in this relationship. They have been seemingly abandoned and left to fend for themselves. Emotions run the gamut. There is anger, disillusionment, and even fear. There is that haunting question of self-worth in the mind of the victim. One becomes introspective and tries to surmise what he might have done to precipitate this abandonment. "Was it my fault?" "Will I ever be able to reorganize and recoup order for my life?" "Am I alone in this?"

Unfortunately, some pastors seemingly abandon their place of calling. They give no clue to anyone within their church that the relationship is about to change. A relationship established through serving the Lord together for years may be coming to an abrupt end. The pastor may have been "courting" another church (or vice versa) and everyone within that church is aware of recent developments, while the church back home is totally in the dark. This way of doing business can have devastating effects upon the church the pastor is about to leave. It is understandable that he does not want to unnecessarily upset his congregation should things not work out with his possible candidacy. But, what happens to his current congregation if a call is extended for him to candidate in another church? Laymen may have the feeling often expressed by the abandoned spouse after an extramarital relationship is uncovered: "Everyone seemed to know but me."

If that does happen, the leaders of the church will be left with the task of dealing with members of the congregation that are experiencing anger, disillusionment, and even fear. Some of this emotional baggage will ultimately be inherited by the next pastor that God brings to a church. Pastors should make the sphere of knowledge as wide as possible. At a minimum, they should keep their deacon chairman apprised of developments that may take them away from their current church.

The Death: Who among us has not experienced death? As a young child I first encountered death when the puppy my father had recently given me became deathly ill and had to be put down. I remember the pain I experienced even as a young child to this day. In the years that followed I lost my grandparents, my uncles and aunts, then my father and my sister. Each time the hurt had to be dealt with within experiential parameters. Did I have a close relationship with the person? Was the death sudden or was it due to a prolonged illness? Was the death due to accidental circumstances or natural causes? Certainly these were always emotional times for our loved ones. Although not absolute, there does appear to be a general pattern of emotions expressed by those left behind. First there is *disbelief* expressed in statements like, "What, how can this possibly be?" Disbelief is often quickly followed by *denial*. "This just can't be happening." "Surely this is not true!" In some cases a person will even express *anger* (as in a divorce) as a result of feeling abandoned. Denial, disbelief, and even anger can be fairly short-lived emotions. Out of necessity they give way to reality, and the person finds himself in a state of *grief*. Sorrow is an emotion that needs to be expressed. Whether in public, private, or both it must be vented. Finally he should find himself in a state of *resolve*. With time, and with God's help, he should be able to deal with the issue that has perplexed his soul. He finds resolution within himself, with his family and friends, and with God. God created each one of us with emotions, and we should not be surprised when we have feelings of emotion. The challenge for us as Christians is to make sure that we allow the Holy Spirit to help us properly control and express our emotions.

While we agree that any sin is bad, what we are faced with in the twenty-first century is the unprecedented proliferation of sin. Today we have at our immediate disposal more information than what any of us can possibly imagine. We can research the annals of history, explore space, tour distant lands, and investigate the most technical fields of knowledge known to man. Likewise, available at our fingertips is the most sensual and grotesque sin that can be expelled from the bowels of hell. What man had to risk viewing in public is now accomplished in the privacy of his own office or at home. Truly, only the Lord knows the breadth and depth of today's problem. Whether on the Internet or through one of the Devil's tried and proven tactics, men are succumbing to sin at alarming rates. Every week men are disqualifying themselves from the pastorate. Tragically played out for all to see is the death of a pastor's ability to minister to his flock. Perhaps the most traumatic transition is the one in which the pastor has sinned to the place that he has disqualified himself from the ministry. His ability to pastor a church had suddenly died.

Even if the leadership of the church has dealt with their pastor's sin in a scriptural manner, they are left tending to the wounds of the membership. From the local congregation throughout the body of Christ there is the initial disbelief, denial, anger, and grief. For some there is a holy anger directed toward Satan for having enticed another pastor into ruining his ability to minister. Many Christians will carry the scars for years as a result of the sins of a man borne out in private. In cases like these even the innocent suffer: sometimes in large number. Joshua 7 illustrates that the private sin of Achan ultimately affected the lives of two and one half million people. Our adversary walketh!

The conditions under which a pastor leaves will have a direct impact upon how the leadership in a church will need to address the needs of the congregation. While you hope that a future transition between pastors will be methodical and painless, it may be instantaneous and agonizing. Your church constitution will be put to the test when the senior pastor's position is abruptly vacated due to sin in his life. During an emotional time like that it should remain clear to the deacon board what their charge is. They should be clinical in their approach, and decisions should not be driven by emotions. Prior to announcing the resignation of the senior pastor, make a priority of determining who is to become the interim pastor. When approaching the congregation with the news of the pastor's resignation, assure them that a plan is in place. Announce who the interim pastor is going to be and communicate what the structure of leadership will be during the interim period. If members have questions, concerns, or need for counsel, they need to know who to approach. Assure the congregation that the deacons and pastoral staff are resolute in the sovereignty of God. He died for the church, and He will certainly guide through even the most difficult times. Use Scripture and the church constitution as your guide. Encourage members to pray and anticipate with open hearts what great things the Lord has for your church in the coming months.

Acts 20:28 reads, "Take heed therefore unto yourselves, and to all the flock, over the which the Holy Ghost hath made you overseers, to feed the church of God, which he hath purchased with his own blood." While this is usually thought of as a verse for pastors, it will become just as applicable to those of you in leadership positions at the onset of an interim period as you begin the search for your next pastor. You are admonished to guard yourselves as well as the flock "over the which the Holy Ghost hath made you overseers" even though that responsibility will be only temporary. Being reminded that His church was purchased by His own blood, you should seek to be only His servants.

3

The Search Committee

Cast thy burden upon the Lord, and he shall sustain thee: he shall never suffer the righteous to be moved. Psalm 55:22

David had personal confidence in the Lord's ability to deliver him out of his troubles. He knew that the Lord saw him in all of his distress and as a result he would continue the practice of calling upon His sovereign name in times of trouble. David's words are similar to Peter's in I Peter 5:7— "Casting all your care upon him; for he careth for you." Had either man given the Lord a reason to turn His back upon them? Surely, but the Lord has promised to watch over the righteous and never to forsake them (Deuteronomy 31:6, Hebrews 13:5).

Those that live righteously can say along with David, "The eyes of the Lord are upon the righteous, and his ears are open unto their cry" (Psalm 34:15). Their confidence in the Lord should be no less adamant than David's. They should know that He sees them in their plight and hears them when they cry unto Him in their troubles. Irrespective of how a pastor has left a church, there is a problem that needs the immediate and careful attention of leadership. Any known sin, and other critical issues, must be dealt with in a forthright and godly manner. Leadership's ability in dealing with any sin that may have caused (or surfaced as a result of) the pastor's resignation will have a direct impact upon the issues inherited by the search committee. Deacons and any assistant pastors on staff should be of one mind and speak with one voice when standing before the church. All differences should be resolved in private. Anything less will sow discord and efforts to find a new pastor will be hampered. If there is not unity present within the leadership ranks, folks may become disenchanted, disillusioned, and discouraged. Some may even begin to leave the ranks. Churches have split and been left in ruins during times like these. The cause is too great to allow any petty issues or egos to get in the way of determining God's will. Remember, our adversary "walketh about, seeking whom he may devour." May you say along with me, "May I be an instrument of service in the hands of the one who died for this church."

Harmony is crucial within the ranks of leadership. It is reasonable to expect that most of your congregation will follow your lead. Sure, there will almost always be some members that are leery and hesitant to follow. Try to understand their predicament. Sometimes the fine line blurs between understanding why people feel the way they do and trying to be an encouragement to them without necessarily agreeing with them. They may not have a better plan; worse, they may not have a plan at all. All they know is that they had put implicit trust in leadership (especially your last pastor) and they have been hurt by his resignation. Leadership's demeanor needs to be scriptural and compassionate. The psalmist points out that "the Lord is nigh unto them that are of a broken heart; and saveth such as be of a contrite spirit. Many are the afflictions of the righteous: but the Lord delivereth him out of them all (Psalm 34:18-19). Allow your members time for their wounds to heal. Being as gentle as nursemaids, work with them and minister unto their needs. If they are being disagreeable, remember that "a soft answer turneth away wrath: but grievous words stir up anger" (Proverbs 15:1).

Your constitution should address how and when your search committee is to be established. This will minimize the possibility of anyone, or group, making a power play in order to accomplish any personal agendas. Committee members should be aware of any minority voice within the church. If there is a problem that can be addressed, seek resolution whenever possible. That an idea is supported by a minority does not necessarily mean the idea is without merit. With the deacons, pastoral staff, and search committee members working in concert, common ground will be established and harmony restored to the body. One of leadership's goals should be to present a harmonious body of believers to your next pastor. In reality this will be possible only in degree. Having a new man as your senior pastor will certainly have a settling effect as well.

Who should be on the committee? Paramount to all other criteria, the men on this committee should be of deacon caliber as outlined in Acts 6 and I Timothy 3:8-13. They should be godly men who are Spirit filled and Spirit controlled. They are men who lead separated lives. In addition to the biblical standards, these men need to be familiar with the major aspects of your church. While each member may not have a grasp of the complete ministry, the committee as a whole should. They must be able to communicate the interests and aspirations of the congregation to prospective pastoral candidates. The committeemen should have a professional demeanor such that they can effectively approach and communicate with contacts that may range from college presidents to laymen in local churches. The men should have a good grasp of the English language and be able to communicate well whether in writing or when speaking. Their manner of dress should complement and lend credence to the authenticity of what they have to say. God's work demands the best! While full-time church staff are undoubtedly members of the congregation, they (especially pastoral staff) should not be considered for membership on the search committee. There may be remote cases in which some of the deacons of a church may be full-time staff. In those cases try to keep the number sitting on the search committee to a minimum.

How many members should be on the committee? Even in a small church there should be a multiple-member committee whenever possible. There should be no credibility to an accusation that the committee is a "one man band." Generally speaking, five seems to be a workable number. Every person on this committee should bear a portion of the load and understand that he will be called upon for individual service for the benefit of the committee. It is easy to overtax members on this committee with the workload. On the other hand, it is just as possible for the more domineering and aggressive members of the committee to overshadow, intimidate, and possibly neutralize input from committee members who have more reserved personalities. The key here is balance. Throughout the life of a committee each man should shoulder part of the load. Knowing the workload is going to be large may be good enough rationale for some to create an even larger committee. There is a point beyond which increased membership leads to counterproductivity. The group can become so large that individuals will begin to question why they are needed on the committee. Procedural issues requiring consensus, such as meeting times, work distribution, visitation schedules, and so forth will become progressively more complicated with additional members on the committee. That point of diminishing returns for the group needs to be determined in advance. A five-member committee may want to consider having an alternate member as well. The alternate should attend all committee meetings from the onset of the search to its conclusion. Should a committee member become ill, get a job transfer, or for some other reason not be able to carry out his responsibilities, there is a man that can step in and play a vital role. Until that time, the committee may choose to seek the alternate's advice, but he should not be allowed to vote. Otherwise, the committee has just grown by one, and there is no distinction between the regular members and the alternate.

What internal organization needs to be established? At a minimum a chairman and a secretary should be assigned for the committee. Involve as many of the five men as possible while assuring the congregation and others that this process is Spirit driven. The deacon chairman already plays a key role within the leadership of the church. It is best that the deacon chairman *not* be the search committee chairman, but he should rightfully be a key player on the committee. He can be the search committee secretary. In that position he speaks on behalf of the search committee, the deacons, and the congregation at large.

When and how often should the committee meet? One church had its committee meet twice a week. On a regular basis they would dedicate one meeting to prayer and the other meeting primarily to business. This format worked well for them. Committees that I have had the privilege to be a part of met a minimum of once a week. Additional meetings were called on an "as needed" basis. Some committees chose to meet every Wednesday during the regularly scheduled evening service. That time was already set aside in the men's busy and overly committed schedules. The committee conducted their own prayer time, Bible study, and business while members of their families attended various programs. Additionally, when members of the congregation saw the committeemen meeting regularly for prayer and Bible study, they were reminded that the committee was being diligent in searching for their senior pastor. Committeemen were praying and fasting throughout the entire duration of the search. A search will not be as trying if there is fervent prayer on the part of the committee and the congregation as well. "Casting all your care upon him; for he careth for you" (I Peter 5:7). Prayer will unify the hearts of the committee members to God, to each other, and to the hearts of the congregation. Over a period of time the hearts and minds of five men will be transformed by the Holy Spirit. The committee will ultimately think and speak with unity.

Which of the committee members should make the reports to the congregation? Communication with the congregation is critical! The committee should agree upon a plan for reporting to the congregation on a regular basis. Congregational members will look forward to hearing these updates. While some committee members may not feel comfortable standing in front of a large crowd, it can be a rewarding experience for them and the congregation. Initially, start with the committee chairman and any others that may be a bit more comfortable with talking with the congregation. Before the report is given, there should be good communication between the committee chairman, secretary, and the deacon chairman. Make sure that the information that is shared with the congregation is accurate, relevant, and does not compromise any assurances of confidentiality. Multiple players speaking on behalf of this committee signal a group effort. When the congregation is informed that the committee is ready to invite a man to candidate, the church will perceive the "oneness" of the committee.

Your church's search committee has been entrusted with the highest possible calling for a layman: the responsibility of finding your congregation's next pastor. What an awesome responsibility! It is a responsibility that your church believes, with the Lord's help, you can accomplish. While already being respected as a godly man, you are about to be driven to new heights in your relationship with your Lord. You already know it will take God's power and His resourcefulness to see this project through to a successful conclusion. Moses spoke to his people as he prepared to transfer the weight of leadership to Joshua. He reminded them in Deuteronomy 31:6, "Be strong and of a good courage, fear not, nor be afraid of them: for the Lord thy God, he it is that doth go with thee; he will not fail thee, nor forsake thee." Encourage yourself, your committee members, as well as your congregation in those truths. Daily search the Word. Have such a close relationship with your Lord that you recognize His presence every second of the day. Capitalize upon every quiet moment in which you find yourself throughout a day and commune with Him. Dedicate everything you are, and everything you are being called to do, to Him. Like David have an open heart with your Lord. Say to Him, "Search my heart and try my reins." Guard your tongue. The writer of Hebrews 13:5 penned, "Let your conversation be without covetousness; and be content with such things as ye have: for he hath said, I will never leave thee, nor forsake thee." Like Paul in Acts 24:16 you should exercise yourself daily to have "a conscience void of offence toward God, and toward men." There should be no unconfessed sin to be found in your life. You have been chosen to be one of the point men in a skirmish in a battle that involves far more than flesh and blood. You can only assume that your adversary will be laying down spiritual land mines in an effort to thwart your mission. Psalm 37:23 reminds us, "The steps of a good man are ordered by the Lord: and he delighteth in his way." **You will be victorious** in carrying out your charge "because greater is he that is in you, than he that is in the world" (I John 4:4). May the Lord bless and direct you every step of the way.

The First Three Months

Be not wise in thine own eyes: fear the Lord, and depart from evil.
It shall be health to thy navel, and marrow to thy bones.
Proverbs 3:7-8

As ambassadors of Christ, and agents for the local church, the men on the search committee obviously need wisdom. They have displayed wisdom in the past, and surely that is one of the characteristics the congregation took into consideration when they commissioned the committee to find them a new senior pastor. The committeemen should remember that they did not become wise by themselves; wisdom comes from God. "For the Lord giveth wisdom: out of his mouth cometh knowledge and understanding" (Proverbs 2:6). The men should be fully committed to shunning evil in their personal lives while being equally determined to seek the mind of God concerning the issues that confront them. Anything less than that level of commitment and they will have a flawed process and outcome (Proverbs 8:13; 14:16; 16:6; Psalm 97:10). Solomon makes it abundantly clear that it is healthy when one is not wise in his own eyes and when he departs from evil. Proverbs 3:7-8 can also be applied to a group of believers who are acting as a body. The search committee can help the church return to a healthy state by finding for them God's man in God's way.

For the sake of further discussion let us assume the following has taken place.

- The pastor is gone.

- He did not leave under the best circumstances and there is some emotional and spiritual turmoil within the church.

- There has been careful communication between the leadership (i.e. deacons and assistant pastors) and the congregation.

- The position of interim pastor has been filled, a job description agreed upon, and his wages set.

- The search committee has been established and commissioned with the blessing of the congregation.

As the deacon chairman, and a newly appointed member of our church's search committee, I felt a great need for godly counsel. This was my first opportunity (and sadly enough not my last) to sit on a search committee. I was a novice at the task of finding a pastor and only the alternate member on the committee had any prior experience in a pastoral search. I knew there was little room for error. I spoke with several deacons and pastors that had experienced a pastoral search. I gained valuable insight as they shared with me procedural techniques that they knew to be effective. I held Dr. Harry Love, state director of the Independent Fundamental Baptist Association of Michigan, in the highest regard and valued his input. Our church membership valued his wisdom as well, since he had assisted our church in the past.

Dr. Love shared with me some general principles that he felt would help our committee when they first met. First, he said, "Go slow!" "God pays dividends for patience." Don't be in a hurry. How many times have you heard that God's timing is perfect? The natural reaction for your committee will be to find a replacement as soon as possible. Finding a replacement is easy. You could have a senior pastor under contract before the week is out. Finding God's man may require a bit more time. Dr. Love's second piece of advice was to have an interim for the church of at least three months after a pastor has resigned. During that time no candidating should take place. Utilize visiting speakers or assistant pastors. The only possible exception would be if the assistant pastor would consider candidating for the position of senior pastor. If that is the case, he should not make it known that he is interested in the position for at least three months. Dr. Love went on to explain that if there were a possibility that the assistant pastor might be interested, there was no need to be in a hurry.

You can assume that there will be some emotional fallout from the previous pastor's resignation. Emotions must not be a compelling factor in determining your next pastor. Emotions should play only the most insignificant role in deciding who God's choice is. Bear in mind the emotions experienced with a pastoral/congregation separation discussed in chapter 2. They may be similar to those experienced in a divorce or death. Dr. Love said that the first three months provide the time needed to mourn the loss and begin to refocus attention upon a sovereign God. It provides a necessary buffer between two distinct phases of your church's history. God has more influence on pastoral movement than we mortals could even imagine. Moses could lead the tribe of Israel only so far before God had him relinquish his position of leadership. It was then up to Joshua to lead the tribes into the Promised Land. Something similar may be taking place in your church.

While continuing to receive counsel from Dr. Love, I was also able to sit down with Dr. Wayne VanGelderen, who was then pastoring Marquette Manor Baptist Church in Downers Grove, Illinois. Dr. VanGelderen had several additional suggestions. He stated, "Pursue only one man at a time until either the man or the church accepts or rejects the proposal." He went on to share, "This must not turn into a beauty contest." He strongly suggested that we not parade a group of pastors before our congregation and then let the congregation pick their "favorite." To the fullest extent utilize your search committee. They should pray, do their homework, and present to the congregation one man for consideration. He went on to say that if the assistant and the search committee were in agreement, the assistant pastor should get the first opportunity to candidate. If the assistant pastor does not wish to candidate, he must go before the congregation to state his decision. This will have the effect of erasing all doubt from the congregation as to what the assistant pastor's intentions are and what he believes his calling to be. Going public will put everyone on the same page and thus reduce the likelihood of confusion.

Both Dr. Love and Dr. VanGelderen were adamant with their next piece of advice. If the assistant pastor decides to candidate for the position of senior pastor and either fails to get the minimum congregational vote required by the church constitution or, after receiving more than the minimum number of required votes, rejects the offer to become the next senior pastor, he needs to immediately resign his assistant pastor position. Further, he and his family will need to leave the church immediately.

At first this advice was difficult to understand and accept. It seemed cold and insensitive. Both men went on to share how it would be nearly impossible to bring any viable candidate before a congregation in which the assistant remained at his post (or in the pew) with a group of supporters that believed he should be their next senior pastor. Both men relayed examples of church splits after such a scenario had played out in other churches. Dr. Love made the point that the ministry is bigger than any one of us. This may prove to be one of the first tests as to the unity of your search committee. If consensus cannot be reached on this point, it is not going to get any easier later in the process. The present and future spiritual health and welfare of your church is at stake. When the search committee approaches the assistant pastor with the option to candidate, make sure he *completely* understands the rules of engagement. Leadership's expectations regarding the assistant and the choice he needs to make should be clear and firm. The assistant may want to use the search committee as a sounding board prior to making a decision about candidating. While that would be an acceptable practice, allowing the assistant pastor to poll the congregation should not be an option. Such an action can sow discord among the believers. This can happen even if that is not anyone's intention. *A partially informed congregation must not be pitted against a fully informed search committee.* The committee needs to be discreet. It should never become a forum for political posturing but rather a tool for determining the will of God. For the church congregation and the search committee to move on to the next phase of calling a pastor, resolution regarding the current assistant pastor's choice is mandatory.

Initial Duties

During the first few meetings, the search committee should concentrate on several different tasks.

- Establish which men will fill the officer positions on the committee. The search committee chairman should, among other duties, lead the weekly meetings and be the person that usually speaks to the congregation on behalf of the committee. While the responsibility of making monthly congregational reports may be shared among committee members, any major developments should be reported by the chairman. The deacon chairman will monitor the progress of the search committee and keep the deacon board informed. The secretary will need to establish a procedure for making and distributing copies of all written communications to the committee members. Keeping minutes of weekly meetings may be helpful. Some committees find that keeping records of only the most important discussions is sufficient.

- Determine regular meeting times and dates. As a general rule the desired length of individual meetings should be agreed upon and then adhered to as closely as possible. You can always call another meeting. Not knowing when God will choose to give you your next pastor, you will want to pace yourselves. This could be a sprint but more than likely it will be a distance run.

- Decide where the meetings will take place.

- Discuss the issue of confidentiality. The men on this committee, not their friends or family, have been commissioned to find God's man for the pulpit. Determine from the onset that discussions held within your meeting room will stay there. If the circle of knowledge is ever to be widened, it should be done so with the knowledge and approval of the committee. Within the ranks of this committee, be prepared to address any breach of confidentiality.

- Pray as if prayer alone is going to usher in your next pastor. Prayer should be constant in your personal life and thereby reflected in your meetings. "Be careful for nothing; but in every thing by prayer and supplication with thanksgiving let your requests be made known unto God" (Philippians 4:6). Your committee may choose to focus a couple of Bible studies on the topics of prayer and fasting. Some committeemen have chosen to fast a day per week for the duration of the search. Some have fasted a meal per week on a regular basis, and another gentleman fasted over a week while he waited on God for a specific answer to prayer. If, when, and how long a man fasts is between him and his God. Men should be encouraged, not pressured, into fasting. Your committee will answer by your actions the question of how important you think God's help is in locating your next pastor. You can find a man for the pulpit on your own. You can have a man under contract and in the pulpit within the week. But to find God's man demands individual and corporate prayer that is humble yet bold, fervent yet constant. Every detail considered, letter written, phone call made, and visit conducted need to be bathed in prayer. You must seek His mind on every issue that is forthcoming and know with full resolve when you have His answer. Expect an answer! Be willing to wait for that answer.

- Open each meeting in prayer and then have a time for the study of God's Word. Both prayer and Bible study will help set the stage for discussions that follow. Have your committee focus its study on how the Lord describes godly leaders and most specifically what the attributes of a pastor should be. Appendix E offers some suggested Bible references for qualifications of a pastor. Study five to six verses per week. Your committee may designate one man to study, prepare, and deliver the weekly lesson. More productive is to share that responsibility among all members of the committee. Irrespective of how busy any particular member may be, it is spiritually beneficial to share the duties. This activity should take place during your entire search. You will find that studying His Word aligns your expectations of a pastor with His requirements. These verses that have been studied will become the benchmarks for evaluating pastors that will be considered by your committee. Whoever is presenting a Bible lesson should have a hard copy of the lesson created that the men can follow and keep for future reference. Appendix E also has an example of a weekly lesson. For the sake of continuity the committee should agree on the amount of time designated for the Bible lesson. What one man might take five minutes to deliver another might require forty-five minutes. The time spent must be productive. Most Bible lessons should be delivered within a fifteen minute time frame. Anything less than fifteen minutes may not be sufficient time for the presenter to share what he has learned from God's Word. More than fifteen minutes and you may find the time once allocated for business is now cut short.

In subsequent meetings consider the following issues that may be worked on concurrently.

Creating a Committee Notebook

Not everyone on your committee may be as organized or detail-minded as the secretary. It is important that the committee members be kept organized and have at their disposal historical as well as current information germane to the search. Have the committee secretary create a notebook for each committeeman. Have the notebooks ready to be handed out at the first scheduled meeting after officers are selected. Two-inch-thick three-ring notebooks work well. At first the notebooks may appear to be too large, but you will be surprised at how they will begin to fill. Design a nice cover page for the outside of the notebooks with the name of your church and committee on it. (See example in Appendix A.) A picture, logo, or Bible verse may be added. The notebooks should be designed to fit your committee's needs and will be for their eyes only. The notebooks should be carefully maintained to guard against those who might be too inquisitive. A typical notebook may include the following sections:

- Notes—Include approximately twenty pages of lined paper for general note taking.

- Bible Studies—After a weekly lesson is taught, store the lesson in this section of your notebook. It is nice if the lessons are typed and three-hole punched *before* the lesson is delivered. Your time is better spent discussing issues rather than punching holes in paper. These lessons will make good reference material in the weeks to come.

- Procedures—It is good to have a summary sheet of the procedures that your committee has agreed upon as standard operating procedures.

There may be times when you will need to pause to refocus your efforts. These pages should include succinct statements summing up agreed-upon methodology. (See example in Appendix L.) Typically this segment of your notebook will be very small.

- Communications—There will be written communications ongoing between your committee and others. Every committeeman should have a copy of every written document that has been sent or received by the secretary. The secretary should present to the committee written documentation highlighting any telephone or face-to-face contacts he has had outside of the committee. This should become part of the secretary's weekly update.

- Résumés—As résumés begin to arrive, channel them through the secretary. He in turn will make copies for each of the members while retaining the original in his file. Committeemen should receive a copy of every résumé submitted to the church. After adequate time has been allowed for reviewing a résumé, it should be discussed at committee level. It is helpful if the secretary provides brightly colored, punched sheets of paper for the committeemen to use to separate the résumés in their notebooks. During meetings, when time is at a premium, the men will be able to more quickly reference résumés being discussed.

- Status—As the search continues, the "status" section will become more important. Names collected will begin to fall into categories: Active, Not Yet Active, and Rejected. As your committee rejects men from further consideration, the secretary should note in the minutes the rationale for rejection. Documenting this information may prove useful when someone on the committee has a question at a later date.

Making Initial Contacts

During the first month, your committee should begin discussing what personal characteristics are important in your next pastor. These are characteristics that go beyond the scriptural mandates. Be careful not to create an atmosphere of debate among yourselves. Rather, generate a climate in which all members can share their ideas and feelings openly. You may choose to precede this discussion with a committee assignment. Give each committeeman until the next meeting to formulate a list of characteristics that he believes should be found in your new pastor. See Appendix B for a sample of one man's response. At the beginning of the next meeting collect and duplicate each man's list and hand the copies out to the committee. Each man should briefly go over his list while the others just listen. Encourage discussion *only after* all the lists have been presented. Look for similarities. There should be some common ground. By consensus, refine the men's lists into a committee list of approximately a half dozen characteristics that can be agreed upon by all the men. This exercise should be done prior to making any contact with the "outside world."

As soon as it is known that there is a vacant pulpit, recommendations will begin to pour in. You should be cautious of, and certainly not initiate, a recommendation from anyone who does not have firsthand knowledge of your ministry. Men to consider are missionaries, pastors, evangelists, and personnel from Christian colleges and mission boards. Again, these should be contacts who have personal knowledge of your church. These men will almost always ask, "What are you looking for?" Having done the previous exercise, the secretary can speak with authority as to what characteristics the committee would like to see. Make your initial contact by letter. (See Appendix C for a sample letter.) Send out about a half dozen inquiries and wait a couple of weeks for the responses. Written as well as phone conversations will ensue. Written responses should be duplicated for the committee record. Should the need occur, send out letters to additional men agreed upon by the committee. The secretary should create a document that has the names of all those contacted and the men they have recommended. Also note the source of any additional recommendations that you may have received and who they are recommending. Compile this information in your notebook.

Be open to recommendations coming from your congregation. Any recommendation made should be written and signed by a member in good standing. Ask the member if the person he is suggesting is aware of the recommendation.

Be cautious of any unsolicited résumé or recommendation that comes from a person unknown to your committee. No one should presume to know the will of God better than your search committee and your congregation. For some applicants this may be no more than a job search. However, any résumé or letter of interest that has been submitted to the committee should be followed up with a letter of receipt from the committee. (See Appendix D for a sample letter.)

Create a Church Profile

You will be required to answer many questions that prospective candidates will have about your ministry. Early in the design phase of your search, consider creating a church profile that accurately depicts the ministry and the local community. Chapter 5 is devoted solely to this topic.

Create a Candidate Questionnaire or Profile

Many churches have conducted pastoral searches and have utilized good questionnaires. It will be easier for you to start with a document that has been used successfully and modify it to meet your committee's needs than to create one from scratch. Chapter 6 will go into greater detail and will reference a sample profile included in Appendix F. Your profile should be ready at the end of the first couple of months.

Begin the Search

Continuing in prayer, studying God's Word, and talking with a small group of men that know your need and the pastoral characteristics you've targeted, you begin the search. You lay aside your own personal aspirations to ask God to conform your mind, and the minds of all of the men, to His sovereign will. You work resolutely with hope and patience. As the names of godly men begin to arrive, you are ready to make that first contact with a man that might end up being your new pastor. Keep in mind that the purpose of the search committee is to carry out the work of the church. They do so until they are prepared to bring a candidate before the church. The church, *not the committee*, makes the final decision and extends the call for the man to become the next pastor.

Nehemiah is a marvelous book to read. There are so many similarities between the predicaments and the emotions that Nehemiah faced and those that may confront you. Nehemiah received a report from several men that the walls in Jerusalem were in a dreadful state. The city was left defenseless against enemy attacks. *Has your congregation been put into a vulnerable position?* The report instantly depressed Nehemiah. He sat down and wept (Nehemiah 1:4). *Are there any among your ranks that are disheartened with what they have recently witnessed?* For a number of days Nehemiah mourned, fasted, and prayed to the God of heaven (Nehemiah 1:5; 2:4). His praying was continual (Nehemiah 1:6). *Have you, on behalf of your congregation, been driven to intense and continual prayer?* Fasting, though not a requirement of the law except on the annual Day of Atonement for the Jews, often revealed a person's reaction to a troubling condition (II Samuel 12:16; I Kings 21:27; Ezra 8:23). *While not a requirement for you, have you considered its merit in developing your relationship with God?* Nehemiah constantly combined prayer with preparation and planning. His people trusted God and at the same time they kept vigilant watch over what had been entrusted to them (Nehemiah 4:9). *Have your people been encouraged to trust fully in God? Has a vigilant watch been set to detect the advances of the enemy?* Too often we pray without looking for what God wants us to do. We demonstrate to God how serious we are when we combine prayer with thought, preparation, and effort.

Nehemiah prepared himself for the task that laid ahead. He sought God's help in prayer. He fully utilized the human resources that were available to him, including his intellect, his past experiences, his accumulated wisdom, his position in life, and the people with whom he had come in contact (in this instance, the king of Persia). The walls were completed in fifty-two days (Nehemiah 6:15). *"Miraculous," you say. May Nehemiah be your example as you prepare your heart and take advantage of your resources. Then watch God work!*

5

WHO ARE WE ANYWAY?

*The fear of the Lord is the beginning of knowledge: but fools despise
wisdom and instruction. Proverbs 1:7*

The essence of true knowledge is to fear God. Apart from Him a person will be ignorant of spiritual things. In contrast with those who fear God and have knowledge are fools who despise wisdom and discipline. There are those who humbly fear God and thus acquire true knowledge. Second are the arrogant fools who by their refusal to fear God demonstrate that they hold wisdom and discipline in contempt. Do not profess to be a "know it all." Be open to the advice of others, especially those who know your church well and can give valuable insight and counsel. Learn how to learn from others. While these verses have direct application to your search committee members, the fear of the Lord should be a controlling principle in your church. There are individuals whose actions speak louder than words; this is especially true of a church. If there have been a deep reverence for and dependence on God, church members will have reflected these attitudes both in worship and service during the good times as well as the tough.

The question of "who are we anyway" needs to be answered sooner rather than later by your committee. Men looking at possibly pastoring your church will want all three perspectives of your church: past, present, and preferences for the future. Knowing your church's roots will play an important part in determining where your church is and where it is headed. While many of the initial tasks of the pastoral search are being addressed simultaneously, creating a church profile needs meticulous attention. Going through the process of creating such a document can be a bit tedious and at times appear to be mundane. If your committee does a thorough job creating this document, your time spent will not be wasted. The procedure formalizes in the minds of the authors the dynamics of the church's people, programs, and surrounding community. The profile oftentimes presents very helpful clues to potential candidates who may not be privy to such information. A second benefit is that the committee itself learns and rehearses, in their minds, the information regarding their local church. Don't be surprised that during the creation of the church profile you may learn a few new and interesting things about yourselves.

The church profile can be used in several different ways. When your committee has refined the list of potential candidates down to three to five men, this profile can be offered as an aid, along with other documents, that a pastor may wish to review as he considers the possibility of being called to your church. The most significant benefit of a profile will be borne out during long conversations that the potential candidate has with the representatives of the search committee. It will be unsettling for you and the potential pastor if he asks in-depth questions about your local ministry, and you don't have answers. There is no shame if you don't know the answer to a specific question about your church's ministry. It is, however, very important for your committee members to have an adequate grasp of the current, as well as the historical, aspects of the ministry. Should a pastor have precise questions, write the questions down. Do not trust your memory. Rephrase questions while you are talking with the pastor to make sure that you are correctly hearing his questions. Go to whoever in the church may be able to answer the pastor's questions. Your responses to his questions may be oral or written. Written follow-up documentation is recommended should you speak with the pastor regarding multifaceted and/or in-depth questions.

Your profile should be done in the most professional manner possible. Today it is possible to put together a working document that is Christ honoring and church honoring without going through a commercial printer. With today's access to computers a clean, thorough, and yet concise document can be created. Make sure there are no spelling errors and try to provide primary documents as often as possible. Pages pulled from church archives that are copies of copies (with ghost images caused by multiple recopying) should be retyped, if possible. Remember, how you present your church in this profile will speak volumes about who you are. The very way you choose to present this information may be a determining factor of whether a pastor allows the search process to go to the next level. The church should pay for all shipping costs of the profile to a prospective pastor. Give him a time limit on how long he keeps it.

Consider the following as you construct your church's profile. Compile all of your information in a three-ring notebook. You may wish to purchase the notebook *after* you gather your documentation in an effort to have the right-sized folder. A large notebook with little information found inside sends one message to the reader. A small notebook crammed with paperwork spilling out of its covers sends another. Design an attractive cover that contains a picture of your main church building or other appropriate photo or logo. Include a letter of introduction and welcome (possibly written and signed by the deacon chairman). Make sure the pages are numbered and the topics are reflected in a table of contents. Contents should include but are not limited to the following:

- Give current location of the church and/or school facilities, including an area map as well as a map of the grounds. Simple building schematic drawings may be helpful, if they are available.

- Provide a section on your church's history. To complete this section, you may need to visit a number of the church members who attended during the early years. Also collect information from church archival documents.

- Include a picture or schematic of the parsonage if your church provides one.

- Provide a short synopsis of all full- and part-time pastoral staff members (include the school administrator). Include the pastor's name and age, a photo (maybe a family shot), years of service within the current ministry, college degrees earned or bestowed, current position, and responsibilities. Be brief. Choose a format that requires little narrative and can be easily viewed.

- Share a statement explaining the chain of command within the pastoral and administrative ranks.

- Report the size of the congregation with a breakdown by age, male/female ratios, and the approximate average family income. Reflect whether church membership is growing, static, or declining. Over time does the composition of your congregation remain fairly stable or does it fluctuate due to a highly mobile community?

- Include the current and last year's annual budgets. Make sure to include faith promise giving statistics. Include the last quarterly financial statements, including total church indebtedness. Share time lines and strategies for paying off any loans. If your church is debt free, disclose that.

- Provide a list of mission boards utilized or approved by your church, current missionaries supported, and to what extent they are underwritten financially.

- Include the most current annual report and any departmental reports.

- Insert the most recent weekly bulletin.

- List evangelists and guest speakers who have spoken at your church in the last few years.

- Describe your church's youth programs, including any camps the children might attend.

- Describe your Christian school (if you have one). Reflect the demographics of leadership, finance, philosophy, curriculum, grades taught, enrollment, and the history of the school. Your efforts here may be simplified by including a current school handbook. Unless requested otherwise, give a global report regarding full-time staff members including numbers employed, degrees held, colleges attended, average age, male/female data, and salaries paid. Include the number of students attending and what percentage of the total student body is made up of children from your local church's families. Include a couple of pictures of the school and activities being held.

- List regional, state, or national organizations your church is affiliated with.

- Share any information that may be relevant regarding current bus ministries (i.e., the number of buses, number of workers, number of those riding the buses).

- Lay out any plans for facility renovation or expansion.

- Give geographic information such as your church's location in perspective to nearby towns or cities. Provide a local map that has a city, town, or county layout. Reflect where most of your congregation lives and works.

- Include a sample of real estate information, including the website addresses of any respected agencies.

- Secure from the chamber of commerce helpful documents that will describe your locale. Their information packet often includes such things as local maps, pictures of museums, college campuses, hotels, hospitals, and opportunities for sports and entertainment activities. If there is heavy or light industry in the area, it will usually be represented within the chamber of commerce documentation. Even the climate may be addressed.

This is not time wasted. Much of the information garnered here will ultimately be shared with a potential pastor once the pastoral search process develops. The bulk of the work in creating your church's profile can be done by someone on the pastoral search committee other than its chairman or those most involved. When you have installed you next pastor, make sure to place this church profile in your church's archives or files. It is a valuable document reflecting your church's total ministry and it can be easily updated in the future.

6

THE CANDIDATE PROFILE

A wise man is strong; yea, a man of knowledge increaseth strength.
Proverbs 24:5

The Book of Psalms shows us God's heart. The Book of Proverbs shows us the mind of God on current issues. Proverbs as a book imparts divine wisdom concerning life. Proverbs 24:3-4 reads, "Through wisdom is an house builded; and by understanding it is established: and by knowledge shall the chambers be filled with all precious and pleasant riches." Wisdom provides security, prosperity, and, as verse 5 points out, additional strength to accomplish the tasks that confront us. Solomon shares with us that a wise man is not self-reliant but will rather look to the counsel of others (Proverbs 11:14; 24:6). Knowledge, wisdom, understanding, and strength are attributes that need to be a part of your spiritual makeup and repertoire. Believing that God is the true source of each of these attributes should encourage you constantly to call upon Him.

I can vividly remember the first time I was called upon to create a questionnaire that would be sent out to prospective pastors. On behalf of our search committee, I searched the church's central records for documents that might have been used for pastoral searches from years past. What I found was a single sheet of questions on a faded and tattered sheet of paper that had obviously been in the file for decades. The paper contained about a dozen simple questions regarding a person's beliefs. There were no questions of any depth whatsoever. Had we used these questions as our sole questionnaire, I am sure that we would have been left with all of our prospective candidates in a dead heat after the profiles had been returned. Generally, it would have been an exercise in futility and possibly a waste of precious time. Creating a candidate profile will prove to be increasingly more profitable as you seek answers to questions that are introspective and probing. This type of profile will be more inclined to reveal the true nature, character, philosophy, and practice of the man that your committee has focused their attention upon. It will help your committee to discriminate between the prospective candidates.

While researching the possibilities of developing a profile, our committee looked to pastors and deacons. We talked with men within our church that had some experience in calling a pastor. We also sought advise from men with whom we had great rapport in other churches. Some pastors shared excellent questions that they thought needed to be asked. One pastor was most helpful. He shared questions that should have been asked, but were not, in a recent interview he had had with a church. With feedback from these and other sources our committee was able to create a profile that specifically met *our* needs. Use the profile in Appendix F as a catalyst in the process of creating your own document. A slightly different rendition of this document was shared with us and similarly we have shared this document with a number of other churches, university students, and professors over the years.

First, your search committee should begin to go through draft reviews of the profile and discuss the value and merit of *every* question being considered. Be sure that the attributes that your committee has targeted as desirable pastoral characteristics are addressed somewhere in your profile. Ask yourselves if the concerns and needs of your current ministry and programs are being addressed. It is not uncommon for an applicant to try to read into the questions and answer with what he thinks the church wants to hear. Remind the prospect that this is not a questionnaire about your church but about him. As a committee try not to tip your hat. You should make every effort for your profile to be

- Uniquely designed to address the issues your committee regards as important.
- Well thought out and presented.
- Easily read and understood by the respondent.
- Thorough but not repetitive.
- A quality document with no spelling, spacing, or punctuation errors.

Present quality, and expect quality in return. In effect, what your committee is expecting from the pastor prospect is absolute honesty and transparency. This can be a threatening and intimidating experience as a man considers whether he is going to complete your profile. Assure the pastor that any confidential information he shares will be kept that way by your committee. Do not betray his confidence!

I once knew a doctor in a small rural Michigan town who had served as a medic in the U.S. Navy during World War II. On the walls of his examination room were vintage World War II posters. One poster I remember most vividly had a sailor with a frantic look upon his face struggling to stay afloat as his ship was sinking in the background. The phrase at the bottom of the poster read, "A slip of the lip will sink a ship." You must realize that your spiritual battle is similar to the battles of war. Understanding the absolute need to protect confidential information, the committee must never breach that level of security. The inadvertent communication of confidential information can have devastating effects. If you are looking for a pastor, you are undoubtedly aware of the spiritual and emotional casualties within your ranks. There can be even more casualties if your committee is not extremely careful with entrusted confidential information.

Information regarding any criminal record and/or moral indiscretion is one example of confidential information being requested (see Appendix F). In the state of Michigan it is necessary to gather such information on a potential employee prior to his being able to work in the public schools.

There are probably similar checks conducted in other states. It is a fair question to ask a potential pastor. Some counselors suggest that it may not be unreasonable even to go through the process of having your candidate fingerprinted for the purpose of a background check. To some this may seem offensive, but we are to the point in America that we need to exhaust every avenue of information about a man and his previous ministries.

A request for a current credit report is also important. One respected pastor commented, "You should not be as concerned with the level of a candidate's indebtedness as you should be with whether he pays his bills on time. Rest assured, if he doesn't pay his own bills on time, he will not make that a priority for the church once he is your pastor." Return of this information should not be an option. Require it of all applicants completing a profile. Take any questions or concerns the committee may have after reading his financial analysis, and ask the pastor for his response in writing. As a common courtesy, the committee should reimburse the pastor for the cost of securing this information. The charge is between $8 and $15. Have all credit information sent directly to the committee secretary. He in turn can make an oral report to the committee at large. Assure the pastor that copies of his financial statement will not be made due to the highly sensitive information that these reports contain. After the information has been secured and shared with the committee, **destroy the report**. That way it can never fall into the wrong hands.

Once your committee has finalized the format of the profile, you are ready to send it to a couple of men being considered. Because of the in-depth nature of the profile itself, do not have every man submitting a résumé fill one of these out. Your committee should be at a place that you are asking the Lord to help you focus your search on no more than five men. Have only those men complete a candidate profile. They should understand that your committee will review their documents and get back with them if there are any further questions or need for clarification. The pastors also need to understand that this returned profile is critical in helping your committee narrow its search to one man.

Be cognizant of the effort and time it is going to take on the part of the pastor completing the profile. Allow two to three weeks for the return of the profile. If there are extenuating circumstances in the pastor's schedule, be tolerant. Remember, he must maintain his regular daily schedule as well as respond to your profile. When sending a pastor the profile, include a letter outlining the committee's expectations regarding time lines and so forth. See the letter in Appendix G as an example. Expect the man to be prompt, thorough, and complete in his answers. When and how he responds to the profile may be as important as what he says. Be understanding about any circumstances that may have compromised time lines or possibly even quality; however, tolerate no dishonesty. Immediately drop from further consideration any man that is not absolutely honest or intentionally less than complete in his answers. Again, he must be blameless.

Preferably the candidate should submit the finalized profile straight to the designated individual on your committee. There may be a time when he may mail it directly to the church, but there should be a close working relationship between the search committee secretary and the person in charge of the church mail. Stress from the onset that all communications between your committee and men in the field (and vice versa) should be considered confidential. As a rule, all incoming mail designated for the committee's attention should be delivered unopened to the committee secretary. Preferably all telephone, e-mail, and fax transmissions should be made directly to the committee chairman or secretary. As much as possible, your committee should maintain direct lines of communications with the pastors.

Once you have received a completed document, drop the pastor a short letter thanking him for the time and effort he put into this task. Assure him that his answers will be reviewed completely and that the committee will get back with him if there is any need for clarification. Give him an idea of what the committee's time line is. You asked him to honor your time line by responding promptly. Honor him with a timely communication as well. Also keep in mind that if he is a respected man of God and has made his intentions known that he might possibly consider a new work, other churches will undoubtedly be making contact with him. If the man is definitely not to be considered any further by your committee, communicate that promptly to him. Be considerate and gentle. He is no less God's man. At this time he is just not God's man for your church, but he is for another work. Both the pastor and your committee have been seeking God's mind in all of this and you have tried to keep this on a spiritual plane. But, there can still be a real sense of disappointment (on either or both sides) when you realize it is not to be. Insensitivity on anyone's part can make a difficult situation worse.

Keep all profiles until the pastoral search process is over. It is possible that God will ultimately have you present to the church a man that was not the committee's first choice. Maintain a high level of communication between the committee and all of the men who have submitted profiles until either side has definitely ruled out the possibility of the man becoming your next pastor.

7

The Search and the Wait

But they that wait upon the Lord shall renew their strength; they shall mount up with wings as eagles; they shall run, and not be weary; and they shall walk, and not faint. Isaiah 40:31

It seems one of the most difficult things for man to do is wait. I mean wait on anything! Impatience is not a trait that has to be taught. It happens naturally and at a very young age. One can recognize some of the earliest signs of impatience by observing the children in the church nursery on a Sunday morning. Better yet, check them out on Sunday night when they're a bit tired from a full day of activity. We might be tempted to overlook such behavior because of a child's tender age. Left to ourselves that impatience continues to develop. Signs of impatience permeate our society. If we are required to wait in a line at a local business establishment for any length of time we soon grow intolerant.

The partner in crime with impatience is inconvenience. We have our own plans and timetables for accomplishing our goals. We are bothered and perplexed by anything that may thwart our endeavors. How sad it is that we are sometimes just as impatient with the one who created us and died for us on the cross. We take our needs and petitions to our Lord. If we find ourselves having to wait for an answer to a specific prayer, we soon grow weary. Doubt begins to set in. We may doubt the effectiveness of our prayer or the one to whom we took the prayer. While sin in our lives blunts the effectiveness of our prayers, never underestimate the capability or concern of our wonderful Lord.

The Jews of Isaiah's day were under the threat of Assyria and later the domination of the godless empire of Babylon. Isaiah knew that unlike pagan idols his God watched over those believers who remained true to Him. Their Creator never grows weary. He undergirds or gives strength to those who grow weary or become weak. Remain faithful to the task to which you have been called and rest assured that you too will be able to endure. You will be uplifted emotionally and spiritually and empowered to complete your task of finding a pastor.

In God's Word there are so many examples of men that made themselves available to the Lord. When the need for a search committee became evident did you ask the same question as David, "Is there not a cause?" (I Samuel 17:29)? Armed more with confidence in his Master than strategic weaponry, David saw the task through to a victorious completion. Plan your strategies well! But ultimately your ability to find God's man resides in the strength of the one who sent you.

By now you have your interim pastor in place, have created a church profile, and have a final draft of the questionnaire that you will be sending to potential candidates. You may have already received some recommendations.

From your congregation: If you get a recommendation from someone in your congregation, secure a résumé from the man who was recommended. Do not automatically disregard suggestions that come from someone in your church. Treat that recommendation with respect and follow through with making an initial contact with the man. If your committee doesn't contact this individual, the stage is set for an accusation to come from the congregation that their voice is not being heard.

From unsolicited résumés: Some man may have heard that there is a pastoral position open at your church. Ascertain, if possible, how he heard of the vacancy. If he was encouraged to contact you by someone who knows your church, and you know that person and appreciate his stand, consider the recommendation and résumé. Be cautious of any résumé that comes in with no direct connection with your church. There are those who are actively looking to relocate and land a new job. To them this is not much more than a job search. Your committee is operating on a higher plane. You are not just looking for a man to fill the pulpit. You are in search of God's man. There is a world of difference between the two.

From the select group of men that you personally contact: The list of characteristics that you are looking for in a pastor has, you hope, helped these particular men in submitting several names for your consideration.

The committee secretary should take all names submitted and create a "Prospective Candidates" sheet with the names of the men recommended and the persons making the recommendations. You may want to place an asterisk next to the names of the men to whom you have sent a candidate profile. A double asterisk can signal the return of that document. As your committee decides that certain men should no longer be considered for the position, your secretary should (1) note the names on the bottom of this same form, (2) include a brief rationale for disqualifying them from further consideration, and (3) list the name of the person who provided the information that led to moving these individuals to an "inactive" list. A person's name being placed on the inactive list does not preclude the possibility that the man may be given further consideration at a later date. You will find this sheet extremely helpful in facilitating committee discussion. The men can see in capsule form your various stages with all of the potential candidates. The sheet will additionally provide a historic picture of where you have been in the process of contacting men. Because this sheet may be updated on a weekly basis, put the date of the most current form in a conspicuous place near the top. You want to be certain that everyone is looking at the most recent form. When updating this form, the secretary should collect all outdated forms and destroy them. This information can be very damaging if it falls into *any* hands other than those in your committee. Shred the old sheets if possible. They contain critical information, some of which is subjective and unique to your ministry. The results of another church's search committee may be completely different. A pastor may not be God's choice for your church, but he may be for another.

From your "Prospective Candidates" list, your committee should seek to limit the search to about five men. These men will be contacted and offered the opportunity to complete a candidate profile and will comprise the "candidate pool." The committee will carefully consider the information provided by these men. The committeemen will prayerfully narrow their search to three and ultimately one man. If the committee and the man are in agreement, he will be given the opportunity to candidate before the church. Remember, it is generally appropriate for your assistant pastor to have the first opportunity to candidate. If he chooses to do so, go slowly. Take several months for things to settle within the church. The committee should proceed with creating a candidate pool even if the assistant plans to candidate. If, for whatever reason, he does not become your next pastor, your committee is prepared to move on.

Make Your Contact

Prior to making any official contacts with potential candidates, the committee should agree among themselves who will be making the contact. That person should be someone who is well informed and can adequately articulate the process of the search as well as the needs of the ministry.

1. Your initial contact will almost always be by phone. In advance, plan your conversation carefully. If you place a call to the pastor's church, be very discreet in what you share with a secretary. If you have the pastor's home phone number, you may want to contact him there. The pastor you are contacting may be totally unaware of any of the details precipitating your call. The time you have chosen to call may or may not be a good time for him to talk. Be sensitive to his schedule. After introducing yourself, simply ask him if this is a good time or if he prefer you to call back. When given the opportunity, briefly explain that your church is without a pastor and your committee has been given his name for consideration.

2. At this point you will try to find out if he is approachable. Begin with a statement like, "If you know that you are where God wants you to be and are satisfied that you are in the center of God's will, then there is no need to go any further with this conversation." If he says that he is where God wants him to be, praise the Lord together and politely terminate the call with best wishes.

3. If he is approachable, then proceed by briefly sharing with him the procedures your committee is following. He will need some assurances. Share your intent to mutually seek the mind of God. Inform him that your congregation will consider only one man at a time. This must not be turned into a "beauty contest." Do not be surprised when you hear a sigh of relief from the pastor. Assure him that you are willing to be absolutely honest and transparent about the ministry you represent. Answer any questions he may have forthrightly and accurately. Hide nothing from this man. There are too many stories of pastors accepting a call only to find a "skeleton in the closet" once they settle into their new office.

4. Explain that your committee has created a candidate questionnaire that you would like to have him complete. Let him know what your time lines are. Balance your need for the returned document with his hectic schedule. Note his ability to work within the prescribed deadlines. Suggest to him that if he should have any questions or concerns while completing the profile, he may contact you prior to submitting the document.

5. Share with the man that the next step in the process is to create a candidate pool of about five candidates. Your committee intends to narrow that list to one man who will candidate.

6. Follow up your telephone conversation with an immediate letter (see example in Appendix G) along with the profile you have drafted.

Narrow Your List of Candidates

The committee secretary should make copies of all returned documents for each member of the committee. Some applicants will provide secondary documents that they feel will help the committee make their decision. It will be helpful if prior to the committee meeting the secretary has gone over every profile checking the document for the completeness of the responses. When a profile has been received, it is helpful if the committee is given time until their next meeting to thoroughly study the document. Have the committee members highlight desirable characteristics as well as items that may be of concern to you. Also note any areas that you may need to seek follow-up information before proceeding further. If any segment of the profile has been left incomplete, contact the respondent and ask him to supply the needed information. Ask him why he didn't complete the profile. Weigh his answer carefully. Through prayer and consultation your committee should agree on the premiere candidate. Pursue that man until God closes all the doors.

Check the References

A list of questions that will be asked of every reference being contacted should be drafted. Having a set of standard questions will aid the committee when making a comparative analysis. Secondary and spin-off questions can be asked on an as-needed basis. Feel free to contact secondary resources but remember to use discretion. These are folks that should be able to speak to the character and professional practice of the applicant. All references to be contacted, including secondary references, should be agreed upon by the committee. Not all members of your committee may be making the reference calls. If possible, utilize committeemen that have expertise in this area. Information collected should be carefully documented and reproduced for all members of the committee.

Conduct a Job Interview

A job interview occurs when two or more individuals meet to discuss the possibility of the future employment of an applicant. Both parties are looking for an alignment of expectations. Types of interviews generally differ only by degree of formality and by the number of participants involved. **Be prepared!** Discuss in advance what roles the different interviewers will play. Divide predetermined questions among the interviewers, and ask all to take notes.

1. An interview can be conducted by a single member of the committee (i.e., committee chairman, deacon chairman, or secretary) either on the phone or in person with the potential pastor. These interviews are typically more relaxed and informal.

2. Several members of the committee may visit with the man and possibly his wife. This interview can be done either in person or via speakerphone. Again, these sessions are fairly informal.

3. The entire search committee may have follow-up questions related to the submitted profile or reference checks. A conference call is a very useful technique to interview a man. It is a great way, short of actually meeting face to face with someone, to begin to really get to know him. The tenor of a man's voice, spontaneity of answered questions, and ability to address difficult questions will help as you get to know the man. Rest assured he will be doing the same as he speaks with your committee. It is exciting to watch as the Holy Spirit begins to bond spirits between your committee and a particular candidate. In this interview there is more structure and more formality, but some levity is healthy as well.

4. Your search committee may desire to set up a meeting between the entire deacon board and the candidate again via speakerphone. A meeting of this nature is often beneficial. In advance he should be aware of, and in agreement with, the nature of this call. It will be the chairman's responsibility to moderate the session, insuring a natural flow to the conversation. Instruct your deacons to sit close to the speakerphone, introduce themselves by name prior to each question or comment they make, and speak clearly and loud enough to be heard. Prior to the call being placed, share with the deacons that this is not meant to be "stump the pastor time." Encourage them to resist the urge to ask the one question that no pastor (or deacon for that matter) has ever been able to answer to their personal satisfaction. The deacon chairman should start things off by asking several questions that he has prepared in advance. Through the session allow follow-up questions to be asked. Make sure that the man is given the opportunity to ask questions of the deacons. Avoid awkward pauses in conversation. After the conference call is

concluded, the deacon chairman will want to moderate a discussion among the deacons as to what their perceptions are. He and/or the committee chairman will want to do a follow-up call with the potential pastor to get his reaction to the conference call as well.

5. Finally, create as many opportunities for dialogue as is practical. Allow for a time when the general congregation is able to ask questions of the pastor. This may be accomplished during the time of candidating.

Contract Approval

Some believe that specific issues of a contract should not be discussed until after the pastor has accepted the call to come. This outlook is not wise. How many godly laymen are willing to uproot their family, sell their home, and move cross-country without an inkling of how they are going to be able to provide for their family? Some pastors would. Other pastors may not. While finances do not drive this process, they are an integral part of the decision that needs to be made. The Lord has enabled your church to be able to offer a certain compensation package. I trust that too has been bathed in prayer.

Discussing a financial package can be a bit touchy. If a man raises the question too early, his intentions may be misread. If he remains silent, he may do so to the detriment of his family. The deacon chairman and/or the committee chairman should discuss finances during a visit with the potential candidate. These two men will have an accurate sense of what the man needs versus what the church is prepared to pay. The topic needs to be addressed by the committee before the man is asked to candidate. This means that the committee needs to do its homework and present to the deacons, for their approval, a contract that can be presented to the candidate for his review. If your committee, your deacons, and maybe your congregation knows what the package is going to be, give the pastor the common courtesy to know as well. Know that both sides are in agreement before he is offered the position. Chapter 8 will go into further detail regarding contracts.

Summary

The search and the wait period can be very short or may extend over several months. The Lord has promised to go with us and empower us as we conduct His business.

I remember one committee meeting most vividly. After months of work we confidently extended an invitation to a man to come and candidate. He asked for two additional weeks to get alone with God prior to making his decision. We took advantage of that time to pray as well. In a meeting prior to the pastor giving us his final answer I mentioned to the men, "Don't be surprised if the name of our next pastor is not even in our notebooks." Later that week the pastor called and humbly and apologetically declined the offer. Determining God's will was the purpose of this exercise. We learned the will of God. Apologies were accepted but not necessary. It would have been a mistake had we proceeded in spite of what we knew God's direction to be.

Our committee was left somewhat in a state of shock. It was as if the Lord were saying to us, "You've done a good job so far; now learn to trust Me even more." Our next pastor's name was not in our notebooks.

"Finally, brethren, whatsoever things are true, whatsoever things are honest, whatsoever things are just, whatsoever things are pure, whatsoever things are lovely, whatsoever things are of good report; if there be any virtue, and if there be any praise, think on these things" (Philippians 4:8).

8

Preparing a Contract

Let the elders that rule well be counted worthy of double honour, especially they who labour in the word and doctrine. For the scripture saith, Thou shalt not muzzle the ox that treadeth out the corn. And, The labourer is worthy of his reward. I Timothy 5:17-18

When a person thinks about preparing a contract for a senior pastor, financial compensation immediately comes to the forefront. While the financial issues are important, other elements of a contract may, in time, have an even greater impact upon the employee. Paul instructs us to faithfully appreciate and support our church leaders.

Too often today's pastors are targets for criticism because members of the congregation may have unrealistic expectations for either the man or his position. A clearly articulated job description is vital. After careful review, you may wish to modify the expectations placed upon the previous pastor. This is where the search committee's prior work will come into play. You've already answered the question "What are we looking for in a pastor?" Are you looking for a preacher, pastor, teacher, church administrator, school administrator, counselor, soulwinner, visitor to the sick or infirm, or combination of the above, and possibly more? A verse for those in a position of church leadership is Isaiah 55:8—"For my thoughts are not your thoughts, neither are your ways my ways, saith the Lord." Believing that to be true, what priority should you place upon the responsibilities of your pastor? Godly men should constantly put the highest priority for the senior pastor on preaching. The message of the cross must be the heartbeat of today's church and its pastor.

How well you treat your pastor can have a direct impact on how long you keep him as well as how easy it will be to replace him. Do your church members enjoy finding fault with leadership, or do they express their appreciation? Does your pastor receive enough financial support to allow him and his family to live without worry? Jesus and Paul emphasized the importance of supporting those who lead and teach us. For further study read Galatians 6:6, Luke 10:7, I Corinthians 9:4-10, and Matthew 10:9-10. Paul exhorts the local church to treat spiritual leaders and elders as men worthy of double honor. Unfortunately, we often take our pastors for granted by not providing adequately for their needs and/or by subjecting them to heavy criticism. As you read this chapter, please consider how you can honor your current or future pastor/teacher.

The committee should review the total compensation package that your church plans to offer its next pastor prior to extending an offer for that pastor to candidate. Dealing with employee compensation can prove to be a touchy topic. Some pastors may require a certain salary even to be considered. Others will testify to their belief that God has in the past, and will in the future, meet their family's needs. Even if the man you're about to ask to candidate reflects the latter view, his needs should be carefully reviewed and met. Erring on the side of generosity is the idea of double honor. There is a possibility that you may find that your search has led you to a man that is financially solvent. His net worth may be beyond that of the average parishioner. What do you do then? The answer is to pay him what the position requires and what he deserves. Pastors that God has richly blessed with financial worth are generally extremely gracious in their contributions back to the local church.

Pastors that faithfully perform their duties are deserving of a decent salary. The key to addressing the salary package the church will offer its next pastor is balance.

A contract that is drawn up without effective research will yield a situation that ultimately leads to stress and strife with (1) the pastor and his family, (2) church members, or (3) both. Church members can become sensitive and even alarmed if finances within the church are tight. Both at home and within the church they may be living from one financial pressure to the next. Do not create a situation in which the pastor and his family are living outside the norm (in either direction) of those filling the pews. Good research on the part of the search committee will yield a total compensation package that is balanced and fair. When you consider wage compensation language, you will need to look

- Within your congregation

    1. Your stewardship officer or church treasurer should be able to give your committee an educated estimate of the average salary of the church membership. He may choose to conduct an anonymous survey of the primary wage earners within the congregation.

    2. Your committee needs to carefully review the current salaries of any other pastors or administrators on staff. The senior pastor needs to have a financial package offered to him that is significantly higher than any of his assistants, irrespective of the assistants' tenure. The senior pastor is the undershepherd of the local church and will be held accountable by God for its development and welfare. What "significant" is must be left to the committee, the deacons, or maybe the congregation. It is best if this can all be taken care of at the deacon level. Congregational discussions regarding any particular staff member's salary may become clouded by the interjection of secondary issues and agendas. Pastors have been hurt by ill-informed members that have spoken their minds during open business meetings. Pastors are not the only casualties caused by those not Spirit-filled. Effective ministries have been blunted and some even terminated as a result of poorly chosen comments made during a business meeting.

    3. It may prove beneficial to take a survey of your deacons' salaries. The average of those salaries may be considered as a starting point in negotiating a compensation package with your pastor.

    4. What is the church's current level of indebtedness and its ability to make payroll and to pay bills on time? Your church treasurer will

again be a valuable resource to you. The church should not necessarily become financially solvent at the expense of the pastor's salary, but on the other hand if God has richly blessed your church, don't be tightfisted with your pastor either.

- Outside your congregation

  1. The committee should conduct a total compensation review of pastors in churches with ministries similar to your own. Preferably the survey should focus on churches within your immediate geographic area. If this is not possible, then your next choice is to target churches with ministries similar to yours, known by your committee, and whose pastor is willing to talk with you openly. It will be difficult for you to make direct comparisons between churches, but this exercise surely will produce valuable information as you reflect upon your pastor's contract. It is here that you need to take into consideration factors other than base salary.

  2. Look at the economics of the church's geographic area. From county and state data determine the per capita income. Look at the cost of living index for your surrounding area over the past several years. This information can be secured from the U.S. Bureau of Labor Statistics or city and county records.

  3. See if there are any periodical reviews of pastoral salaries. While this information may not be a driving force in establishing a contract, the information may prove to be insightful.

Beyond base salary and direct financial compensation are a number of other benefits that need to be considered by the search committee on behalf of your pastor. You may wish to use some of the following benefits as a guide for designing the questions you plan to ask as you research other churches' pastoral compensation packages. The logical point person in making contacts with pastors from other churches is your own deacon chairman. You may detect a bit of initial reluctance by a pastor to openly share his compensation package because, right or wrong, his own congregation may not be fully aware of this information. Rest assured, pastors don't get many calls of this nature. This must be a call in which the sole driving force of the questions is to get answers that will ultimately help your church honor God and your pastor. When our church has made assurances that this information will be used discreetly, to the man, pastors have been most helpful.

The candidate you've contacted may ask you some rather probing questions. It would be wise for you to be well rehearsed in your own church's contractual practices. These may include

Tax Sheltered Annuities: Your treasurer will know what state and federal regulations are placed upon tax sheltered annuities (TSA). Churches will often provide 100 percent of, contribute in addition to, or even match an employee's contribution. There should be room for pastoral discretion and preference here. He may already have a plan in place that he is using to develop a portfolio for retirement. It will also be important to articulate the church's involvement with paying Social Security fees.

Housing: A church may offer the use of a parsonage with or without utilities. This practice has been on the decline over the past twenty years. While a parsonage is an initial benefit especially to a young pastor, that benefit quickly erodes as the pastor builds no equity in his home over time. By the time a pastor retires, he may have nothing but memories and his last check. An alternative to a parsonage is a housing allowance for which the pastor will provide his own residence. This is a difficult alternative for a pastor just graduating from college who has little credit established and little money in his pocket. Help that pastor get established and soon he'll be realizing a growing equity that he'll be able to manage to the benefit of his family. There are certain Internal Revenue Service (IRS) nuances that provide some attractive incentives for pastors to have a portion of their salary designated for personal housing. You may find further assistance when you check with your church treasurer, church financial advisor, legal counsel, or the IRS. An additional suggestion for your consideration would be for the church to offer to pay the closing costs on the pastor's new home as part of his first year's contract.

Car Allowance: A realistic allowance is a bare necessity in compensating your pastor for miles traveled while conducting church business in a personal vehicle. You may further consider providing a church-owned vehicle and gas credit cards. If you choose these options, put into place a system that carefully monitors their use.

Health Insurance: Make sure that you provide Workman's Compensation insurance. Provide the best insurance package that your church can afford that addresses life, medical, dental, and optical. Some churches provide long-term care as well. With an aging population in the United States, and increased medical costs, insurance benefits for pastors must not be left as an afterthought. Negotiate with different carriers for the best coverage. After a period of time don't be afraid to change carriers as long as you don't negotiate the pastor's benefits below acceptable limits.

Library Allowance: Just like a tradesman needs tools, so pastors need reference materials. Occasionally, take your pastor to a Christian bookstore and let him buy what he wants. If some of the books that he desires most are no longer in print, perhaps a trip to a bookstore that sells used books would be like a treasure hunt for him. Assuming that you've provided your pastor with a computer, consider software. There are software packages on the market today that provide reference materials at a fraction of their original price. There are databases complete with multiple Bibles, commentaries, outline programs, biblical atlases, dictionaries, and classic reference texts. All of these can be placed at your pastor's disposal with a library allowance. The greatest thrill for the pastor is having an opportunity to make his own choices regarding his study aids. Also remember that should your pastor move on to another ministry, these resource materials are his. They were part of his compensation package.

Vacation: Provide time for the pastor and his family to be away on vacation. They need time to be with family and friends just as any other member of your congregation. It is common practice for a certain number of weeks of vacation to be agreed to upon initial hire. After several years of service this time should be extended.

Business Days: Call these days whatever you want, but a pastor needs time away from the office in order to attend conferences or association meetings, answer a request to preach in another church, or attend board meetings for boards he may be a member of. One thing that some churches will often build into their contract is a stipulation as to the maximum number of Sundays that the pastor can be out of his own pulpit. This may include, or be in addition to, Sundays missed while on vacation. Once again the key words here are balance and accountability.

Work Week: If you're concerned that your pastor may try to cut short his work week, you are probably considering the wrong man. On the other hand, some pastors will not take a day off. They will sacrifice themselves and their families on behalf of the church. While admirable in the eyes of some and feasible for the short haul, this will take a toll on the man and his family. It will eventually have an effect on his ability to minister to others. A simple sentence in a contract may give a deacon chairman a bit more clout when he suggests to his pastor that he needs to take his day off.

Office Equipment: Make available to the pastor an up-to-date computer, management software, a cell phone, and a pager. All of these may not be necessary or even desired by the pastor, but they should be made available to him for church-related use. It needs to be made clear from the beginning if this equipment is to remain the property of the church.

Educational Expenses: (1) You may want to consider contractual language for paying for any studies that lead to additional degrees. There should be a system built into the contract language for preapproval by the deacons. Paying for course work will be an encouragement for your pastor to constantly be learning and growing. As fresh messages are preached and his leadership in the church is further developed, the congregation will soon realize the benefit of an investment in their pastor's education. (2) In addition, if your church has a Christian school, consider allowing the pastor's children to attend tuition free. (3) One church, for example, puts aside funds that will partially underwrite college tuition for the pastor's children when they are ready to attend a church-approved Christian college.

Moving Expenses: If you believe the man that you're about to hand this contract to is the man that God has called to your church, then help him get there. Be willing to pay all of his moving expenses. Work with him so that the most cost efficient moving company can be secured.

It would be wise when you draft the contractual document to run any major changes past the deacons for their approval. This will be a test for accuracy and efficacy. Also, if after speaking with the candidate, changes need to be made in the contract, share those changes with the deacons. These types of minor negotiations need to be worked out prior to a pastor officially candidating. Things can become quite harried if the congregation has extended a call to a pastor and you still haven't agreed upon the terms of employment. When the candidate accepts the call to be your pastor, present him with two copies of the contract. Have him sign and date both copies. Someone on behalf of your church should also sign and date both copies. One copy will be retained by the pastor and one copy kept by the church treasurer. A good contract will eliminate misunderstandings and hard feelings down the road. See a sample contract in Appendix K.

9

PLANNING THE VISIT

For we are his workmanship, created in Christ Jesus unto good works, which God hath before ordained that we should walk in them. Ephesians 2:10

We become Christians by accepting God's gift of unmerited grace. Paul wrote in Ephesians 2:8-9, "For by grace are ye saved through faith; and that not of yourselves: it is the gift of God: not of works, lest any man should boast." We have *nothing* that we can add to that grace. Like a masterpiece, "we are his workmanship." Our salvation could be fashioned only by God Himself. Praise God He was willing to pay the price to purchase that gift for us. While there is no action we can undertake to merit salvation, God does intend that our salvation result in acts of service. We were saved to serve Christ and the church. Remember that we are eternally indebted to our Master while we prepare to serve.

Visitation will play a crucial roll in helping the search committee determine which man of God the Lord will have them focus their attention upon. Planning a visit will be expedited if the committee has already established what characteristics they are looking for in a senior pastor. If properly addressed, this criteria will be common ground for committee discussion when the previsit and postvisit discussions are conducted. The committee should make sure this procedural element has been taken care of prior to making any visits with potential candidates.

There is another question the committee will need to address before any visitation can begin: "Where are we going to find the funds necessary to underwrite travel, food, and lodging for committee members and pastors that we are about to contact?" There should already be a line item in the church's approved budget for the senior pastor's salary. These funds should not be diverted to some other expenditure. The congregation's charge to the committee is to find a senior pastor. Whether paying a senior pastor's salary or searching for a senior pastor, the money should still be properly expended as per the direction of the congregation in its approval of the annual budget. In the case in which there are multiple pastors in a church, and you have given a raise to whoever is interim pastor, there should still be sufficient funds remaining to adequately conduct a pastoral search. (If you have given an assistant pastor the full responsibility of the senior pastor, then compensate him accordingly with the previous senior pastor's salary during the interim.) In reality, he will probably be doing a job and a half. He'll be carrying out his regular responsibilities as well as his newly assigned responsibilities. It is a common response of newly elevated assistants to gratefully and humbly decline the raise, giving assent to their belief that this is their rightful responsibility in God's service. It is also the God-given responsibility of the local church to properly compensate its leaders. The discussion is generally over at that point. Should that be the case, use the now-abandoned assistant pastor's salary line item as your funding source for securing a senior pastor. The rationale for the interim pastor's salary should not be kept a secret from the congregation. They need to be cognizant of the fact that the deacons are aware of, and appreciate, the efforts of the interim pastor. Deacons, you have an obligation to monitor the needs of your interim pastor. Be sensitive to his physical, emotional, and spiritual needs. With the same regard monitor his family. Hire guest speakers and do some temporary realignment of job descriptions if necessary, but take good care of your full-time staff. Many times the assistants will do this realigning themselves without being encouraged to do so by the deacons.

There are some general rules of engagement regarding visitation that should be discussed prior to making contact with a potential candidate.

1. Pray! Spurgeon penned, "Prayer girds human weakness with divine strength, turns human folly into heavenly wisdom, and gives to troubled mortals the peace of God" (*Morning and Evening*, October 11). It is imperative that the committee as individuals, and a body corporate, be Holy Spirit led throughout this encounter. "Be careful for nothing; but in every thing by prayer and supplication with thanksgiving let your requests be made known unto God" (Philippians 4:6).

2. Plan your visit completely. If you are planning to rent a car, be sure to make arrangements ahead of time. If someone in your group is providing transportation, make certain that you adequately compensate him. On one occasion we had a member of our deacon board that had a pilot's license and owned his own plane. We called upon his services to fly three couples to visit with a pastor and his wife in another state. Whether you are driving or flying private or commercial, the church needs to pick up the tab! It would be prudent to establish a rule within the committee and communicate it to the church treasurer that there will be no reimbursement for funds expended without properly documented receipts. These bills should be accurately itemized using a standard form (even if the form has been created specifically for this search). Your treasurer should be able to produce samples of various reporting formats for you. Choose one and use it. See Appendix M for a sample. Remember that your committee must guard itself in order to be beyond reproach in respect to how you are spending the Lord's money. This does not mean that questions will not come up, but it does guarantee that you will have accurate records and you can speak to any and all expenditures. When you have safeguards like these in place, and the congregation is aware of your thoroughness, few to no questions are ever levied at the committee.

3. The time spent visiting a pastor may range from a few hours to several days. We have had several cases in which we were corresponding with men whose ministries were thousands of miles away from our local church. While we were not yet ready to embark upon a formal visit, God provided opportunities to meet with nearly every one of these men. Sometimes the individual being considered by our committee came within an hour or two's drive of our church. Several pastors and

one evangelist had speaking engagements nearby. Two men were attending missionary conferences, and one was attending a college benefit. Several of the men we went to see were in the area visiting family or friends. God provided the opportunities, but we had to make ourselves available to meet with these men sometimes with very little notice. Have a couple of your men meet the pastor at a neutral and convenient site. If the pastor will have his wife along, it is wise to take your wives along as well. A hotel is a nice place to have one of these kinds of meetings. Your business can be easily conducted if you find a business lounge to meet in private. Provide a meal or light refreshments for all of those in attendance.

4. Make sure that you document well all telephone conversations and written communications before, during, and after the visit. Share this information in detail with your committee.

5. Have a debriefing session after the visit for all of those that make up your visiting team. If at all possible, conduct this debriefing session prior to returning home while your thoughts and experiences are still fresh. Try to encourage even the most shy or reluctant members to share their thoughts on what they have just experienced. When you ask for feedback from each person's own perspective, there are no right or wrong answers. Again share all of this information (positive and negative) at the next committee meeting.

Visitation may range from a fairly private visit to an absolutely "known by all" activity. Use discretion! It is wise for the committee to yield to the direction of the pastor with whom you are planning the visit. He will be sensitive to the needs of his congregation in ways that your committee would never be aware. My father once told me, "Information is cheap, but it pays large dividends." Don't be afraid to ask questions that will assist you in planning your encounter. Some questions you may first want to ask yourself and then the pastor being visited may include any of the following:

- Do you mind if we visit your church?

- On what date would you like us to come and what would be the best time to arrive?

- Do you have any directions for us as to how we are to conduct ourselves during the visit?

- When we attend a service, where would be the best place to park?

- Will there be any members of your congregation who are aware of our visit?

- Where would you like us to sit in the auditorium?

- Do you mind if we attend a Sunday school class? Which would you recommend?

- Do you have a time for introducing visitors during your service? If so, how would you like us to handle that?

- If we are staying overnight, where would you recommend we stay?

- Will there be a time when we men can get together to discuss the needs of our ministry with you?

- Can we plan a time when all of our wives can be together, and will there be an opportunity for us to fellowship as couples?

Before you make your visit, have well established what information you want to secure either from the pastor, from his wife, or experientially through the congregation. Write down any questions that your committee wants answered. This will help guarantee that when you get private time alone with the pastor your time together will be profitable. You must be ready to speak on behalf of your congregation and answer questions about the ministry you represent. By this time you had better be the most informed person in your church. There should not be one aspect of your ministry that you can't speak about knowledgeably. If the pastor requests in-depth reports about your church, make sure you understand his questions and see that he gets a quick and accurate written response. On the other hand, know what questions you need to have answered. Write them down and include them in your travel planner prior to your visit. (Do not march into the church you are visiting with your search committee notebook in hand.) You can always modify your questions as you go through the process of talking with the pastor. Transcribe his answers as he speaks. Initially, this document will be for your eyes only, so you must be able to decipher your own notes. The time allocated for discussions with the pastor is precious. If you have used your best note-taking skills, you will be able to accurately transcribe your notes into narrative format at a later time. Maintain a careful balance between the need for taking good notes and being courteously attentive during your time together with the pastor. Adequate preparation on the team's part will directly correlate to how beneficial your visit will be. You may choose to create a folder highlighting the areas of the ministry you wish to observe, leaving spaces for your comments. You may choose to use a format similar to the one in Appendix H. This visit is costing you, your congregation, and the pastor being visited time, energy, and personal, as well as congregational, funds. Be prepared! The following are aspects you may want to consider as you view the man and his ministry you are visiting. These questions are in no specific order nor are they meant to be all-inclusive. Targeted issues must be left to each visiting team.

- Look at the man as a person, husband, father, and pastor/preacher. What are his goals and expectations for himself, his family, and his church? What is his leadership style? What does he like to do for recreation? If the Lord so leads, when would he see himself being available to make the transition to your assembly?

- What are the thoughts of the wife and children regarding your approaching her husband and their father?

- Look at his home, vehicle(s), dress, and so forth. These may speak as much about how well his current church loves and takes care of him as it does about how he chooses to take care of his family.

- Look carefully at the church grounds, buildings, and facilities. Look at his office. Are they well taken care of?

- Are the people friendly? Do they appear happy? What percentage is male/female? What are the ages of those in attendance?

- Are the ushers courteous and helpful?

- What programs appear to be important to this congregation?

- Is there a youth program? What is the emphasis and how many regularly attend?

- Bring home a church bulletin and a quarterly or annual report if one is available.

- Look at all aspects of the choir, including size, male/female/age breakdown, choice of musical selections, ability to project sound, and ability to enhance the service.

- Consider carefully the sermon. Note the pastor's style and whether the congregation seems to be responsive. If possible, secure a tape of the message and make it available to your search committee. You may want to ask the pastor for tapes that differ in style or format (i.e., from a Sunday or Wednesday evening service).

- Target anything requested by your committee back home while maintaining a high level of discretion.

Your visit will be only as effective as you are prepared. Committeemen making the visit should have prior discussion (even if in transit to the session) reiterating what you are looking to accomplish and the strategies that will be used. Divide the tasks, allowing your team to focus their attention on different aspects of the ministry. If the pastor you are visiting will have his wife in attendance, it will be mutually beneficial to have a couple of the committeemen's wives go along as well. Most pastors are pleased to have their wife meet some ladies from the church making the visit.

Your committee has prayed and planned. It is now time to make "face to face contact" with the man who may ultimately become your next pastor.

10

VISITATION PRIOR TO CANDIDATING

Trust ye in the Lord for ever: for in the Lord Jehovah
is everlasting strength. Isaiah 26:4

A visit can take on a multitude of different forms. One kind of visit is initiated by your church. Some search committees find it more beneficial to visit the potential candidate before he visits their local church. This, of course, is not true in all cases. Another kind of visit is initiated by the candidate himself. A pastor with whom your committee has made contact may be in your area on business. He may stop by for an initial visit with members of the committee or maybe just to sit through one of your church services. In either case, he is no more than a visitor and should be introduced as such. Every visit made will be a unique experience, which is all the more reason for you to be prayerfully prepared and Spirit led.

You Visit the Candidate

The search committee may conduct a visit during the initial stages of getting to know a man and his ministry. Or, the visit may take place as late as when the committee is nearly set to invite the pastor to candidate. It generally is an encouragement to your congregation if you inform them that visits are being made. It is best if you do not share the man's name, church, or even the town you're going to be traveling to. It should be sufficient for your congregation to know that your committee is making contact with available men of God. If you have not done so already, explain to your congregation the rationale behind not disclosing the name of the man or his church. Most, if not all of your members, will understand the reasoning and will respect the fact that your methodology is not up for debate. The stage has been set weeks earlier when the committee chairman stood before your congregation and explained the committee's search methodology. This will serve only as a gentle reminder.

There is a possibility that at some point a sense of helplessness may set in among some members of your congregation. They may want to be of assistance to the committee. They want to be part of the solution in finding a pastor. Keep them informed on at least a monthly basis. You can assure them of the importance of their constant prayer support. Encourage them not to underestimate the power of prayer! In your next monthly congregational update you may want to disclose, *in the most general terms*, the results of your visit(s). As an example, you can disclose that in the past month your committee visited three potential candidates and their wives. You may go on to share that the committee has agreed that there was no need to proceed further with two of the three men, but further investigation needs to be conducted on the third. Share with the congregation that résumés continue to be received and reviewed. Procedurally, it is wise to accept names of potential pastors that your own congregation may recommend. If the membership feels that they have been isolated completely from the search process, they may show symptoms of dissatisfaction. It is helpful if the committee clearly articulates to the congregation that they may submit names of men. All recommendations should be put in writing and signed by the member. The committee may wish to speak with the member making a submission if further information is needed. Obviously, recommendations should be accepted only from members in good standing.

Your committee may be faced with a situation in which a member has already made contact with an individual. The member may even submit the man's résumé on his behalf. Should that happen, express your appreciation to the church member. Follow up with a letter to the candidate stating that you have received his résumé. Also mention that it has been turned over to the committee for consideration. See Appendix D for a sample letter. It can be modified to fit your needs.

Conduct a visit of a potential candidate only after his name has been submitted and discussed by the search committee. Remember that this is a group activity and not the commission of the church to any one individual. The entire committee needs to be aware of the visit and have given its full support for a representative(s) of the committee to make contact with the pastor. Whenever possible it is best if there are at least two committee members present for the visit. It is always good to have a second opinion when you do your debriefing after your visit. When presenting your committee report, do not be afraid to share any differing opinions of those who made the visit. Share all information and all perspectives. This may set the stage for developing very specific questions that will be asked of the potential candidate at a later date. Never overlook the possibility of conference calls, between your search committee and/or the deacons, with the man you are considering as a potential candidate. Invite assistant pastors to sit in on these sessions.

While there can be many variations, following are four different approaches based on how much a potential candidate and his church knows about the purpose of the visit.

No Exposure

- Candidate–is not aware of the visit
- Pastoral Staff–is not aware of the visit
- Deacon Chairman and/or Deacons–are not aware of the visit
- Congregation–is not aware of the visit

This type of visit is helpful when the search committee has been given a name of a pastor that may be considered as a potential candidate but little is known by the committee about the pastor. If you are going to make this kind of visit, limit the number in your party to no more than two. Any more than that and you will draw considerable attention to yourselves, and that certainly is not the purpose of your visit. If you are going to a church with a small congregation, you may want to limit your number to just one visitor. I remember a case in which a pastor's name was brought up in one of our weekly committee meetings. The pastor being discussed had a small church on the other side of the state. As it worked out, the committeeman who introduced the pastor's name for consideration was going to be making a trip to the west side of the state to conduct some personal business. He indicated that he would be able to slip into the church while passing through on Sunday and make a report a week later to our committee. In this particular case the pastor was dropped from further consideration without involving, and possibly upsetting, either him or his congregation.

Partial Exposure

- Candidate–is aware of the visit
- Pastoral Staff–may be aware of the visit
- Deacon Chairman and/or Deacons–Deacon Chairman may be aware of the visit
- Congregation–is not aware of the visit

Most of the visits you will conduct fall within the scope of either partial or expanded exposure. These two approaches vary only in degree. At the earliest stages of communication between a pastor and representative(s) of your committee the degree of exposure is usually very restricted. At this stage neither the man nor your team knows God's will regarding this man becoming your pastor. Pastors generally want to protect their congregations from unwarranted stress and concern. This point may cause the greatest internal apprehension. Who should know about the substance and timing of a visit may be a difficult issue to work through. Then again, it may not. When the pastor knows that a visit is being made, consider the possibility that he share this information with his immediate pastoral staff, including his deacon chairman. They need to understand that a visit will take place as a precursory phase prior to his being asked to candidate. Ultimately, the decision of who knows will rest with the pastor being visited, and your team should yield fully to his direction.

Expanded (or ?) Exposure

- Candidate–is aware of the visit
- Pastoral Staff–is aware of the visit
- Deacon Chairman and/or Deacons–Deacon Chairman, at least, is aware of the visit
- Congregation–is not aware of the visit

If there has been ongoing dialogue between your committee and a specific pastor, it should come as no surprise to him when you bring up the topic of making a visit. If the pastor is aware of the nature of your attendance in his service(s), he probably should make others aware as well. Be prepared for a strained welcome mustered by those "in the know" when you attend their service(s). This is totally understandable and for all intents and purposes acceptable. I have always been treated in a hospitable and friendly manner. These folks undoubtedly love their pastor and want that relationship to continue. To the man, every pastor I have met has had the same feelings of wanting to protect his congregation from harm. Isn't that the kind of heart you are looking for in a shepherd? But, these same pastors are open to the possibility that God may be extending to them a new call. Likewise, their congregation will have to consider making the same kind of visits should God call their pastor to a new work.

Full Exposure

- Candidate–is aware of the visit
- Pastoral Staff–is aware of the visit
- Deacon Chairman and Deacons–are aware of the visit
- Congregation–is aware of the visit

It does not happen as often, but you may enter into a situation in which it is common knowledge that the pastor has made himself open to being approached by other ministries. When this does happen, there are usually some interesting consequences that follow. Some pastors have been able to accomplish this with very successful results even to the point of helping the congregation choose his replacement. More often however, the pastor's ability to lead that congregation begins to wane and in some cases totally erodes. Generally speaking, the sooner he leaves, the less trauma for the local assembly. Most pastors that have agreed to a visit will choose to operate within the design of either partial or expanded exposure.

There are cases in which a resigning (or retiring) pastor chooses to stay in his current church. Unless the pastor severs all responsibility of leadership, the lines of authority will be blurred for the congregation, the staff, and most importantly for the new pastor. Your committee must communicate to your next pastor that he alone is in that position of leadership. The deacons too must pledge their wholehearted support and counsel.

The Candidate Visits You

Undoubtedly, you will find that a candidate's visiting your church is a much easier task to conduct because your committee will be controlling most, if not all, of the itinerary for the visit. There is the possibility that the pastor making the visit may want to visit your church without disclosing to your congregation any of his motives. His only interest in making an initial visit will be for his information only. Committees sometimes forget that this process is a two-way street. You should take advantage of this opportunity to have a time when the visiting pastor can sit down and discuss issues with the search committee. Discussions may include the salary and benefit package you are prepared to offer. You might be interested in finding out what the minimum percentage of yea votes he would require before accepting a call to be your pastor. This would be a terrific opportunity for the visiting pastor to meet with any assistant pastors you have on staff. They certainly have a vested interest in this man. "Can I work with this man?" "Can he work with me?" "Will I be asked to leave?" All of these questions are on the minds of the assistants. The committee may as well find out early on what the intentions of the visiting pastor are. Don't be afraid to pose these questions to him. Again, be mindful of the importance of proper timing with these types of questions. If the assistant pastors have been kept current as to the developments within your committee, they will be ready to meet with this man. Nothing advances a relationship more than quality time spent together. Please understand that up to this point no commitment has been made, by either side, as to the possibility of this man candidating. Both he and the committee will use the information garnered from this visit to help them discern the Lord's will in progressing even further with your committee. Neither his congregation nor yours will be aware of the possibilities that may stem from this visit. Should the man decide not to pursue the possibility of being your pastor, you have saved your congregation (and his) potential heartache.

Because of schedule and travel limitations, there may be limited opportunities for a pastor to visit your ministry. In all likelihood a second visit will be either an "expanded or full exposure" type of visit for your congregation. Prior to the pastor being invited for a formal second visit, all references should be checked thoroughly. Surely, if an applicant has done his homework, you can bank on the fact that his references will give him high marks. With a little bit of discernment on the part of the person checking the references, names may surface of other individuals who can speak to the character and practice of your potential candidate. Primary references have undoubtedly been made aware of the pastor's interest in pursuing this position and are waiting for your phone call. Contacting a secondary reference carries with it a bit more risk. There is the risk of prematurely exposing the pastor's intentions and thereby unnecessarily enlarging the circle of those aware of his activity. Urge the party contacted to keep this call in utmost confidence. You should be able to collect collaborating testimony as to the prospective candidate's character, policies, and practice. If, in the process of checking references, you come across someone who shares information that is troubling, proceed with caution. Given the right opportunity, you might even seek the pastor's reaction to the information you have been given. Being confronted with negative information or accusations will also disclose how he will handle himself in the future when faced with negativism. Do not purposefully create a situation in which you are looking for something negative about this pastor. On the other hand, capitalize on the situation and carefully note the pastor's response. You may find that the person making negative innuendoes is unhappy and disgruntled because of some personal affront. *Be cautious. Be analytical. Be thorough. Again, be Spirit filled and led.* Above all, make finding your next pastor a spiritual undertaking.

After all of the committee's questions about this man have been satisfactorily addressed, all references checked out, and the committee remains in one accord, you are ready (if the pastor also agrees he is ready) to move on to the next step. This can be either a formal visit by the pastor and his wife or the actual process of the pastor candidating for the position of your senior pastor.

11

CANDIDACY

Whether therefore ye eat, or drink, or whatsoever ye do, do all to the glory of God. I Corinthians 10:31

One of the guiding principles to being an effective Christian is to honor God with all that you have, do, and say. That should continue to be a driving force in the life of your search committee as well. His love must permeate motives and actions. Plans are being finalized for a man to candidate to be your next pastor. There are many details that still need to be addressed.

Unless your committee is absolutely unified in their belief that this man should be your next pastor, do not present him for the church's consideration. While recognizing that the man is not perfect, you believe that God has brought him to your church for the purpose of being your next pastor. The deacons have been kept current through all of the events that have led to this point. They too should be of one mind, and give a 100 percent vote affirming their belief that this candidate should be considered for the position of senior pastor. The pastoral staff have been kept informed, and they have taken advantage of multiple opportunities to meet with the pastor. They too wholeheartedly support his candidacy.

The committee chairman should check with the pastor, prior to his coming, to make sure that those in leadership positions at his current ministry are aware of his intention to candidate. If he has not seen to that task, he should. A pastor should not candidate without informing those he presently pastors. That tactic severely undermines the bond of security and honesty that should exist between a pastor and his flock. Surely you would want to be treated the same way in the future. On the other end of the spectrum, a man might actually resign his position in his current church prior to candidating. While the merits of such a dramatic action can be debated, this decision *must not* obligate the congregation for which he is about to candidate.

There are several factors that affect how long the actual candidacy period should last. If the candidate resides near your church, you may want the candidacy period to extend beyond a weekend encounter. He could travel between his current ministry and yours without any great inconvenience. An extended candidacy may also be warranted when the pastor resides a significant distance away from your church. When the cost and time needed for travel prohibits the pastor from traveling back and forth, staying a few extra days may be appropriate. This will provide multiple opportunities for the pastor to meet with people. He will be able to preach several messages including Sunday morning, Sunday evening, and Wednesday evening. An extended stay will also provide more opportunities for the pastor to meet with the staff, deacons, and congregation.

Some churches prefer a slightly more abbreviated format for candidacy. The candidate may arrive and stay for several days but usually less than a week. At a minimum, he should preach Sunday morning, Sunday evening, and preferably Wednesday evening. If your church has a school as part of its ministries, provide an opportunity for the pastor to preach a chapel message. Arrange a special chapel if one is not scheduled during his visit. Having the pastor preach a chapel message has dual purpose. The students and staff members will see the man in a different light, and the pastor will have a better idea of the spiritual tenor in the school. In addition, your committee will need to provide opportunities for every member of the church to meet him. The key here is for maximum exposure during the time permitted. Whether a meeting is formal or informal, one on one or a group, get the pastor before the people. An abbreviated candidacy can be as beneficial as an extended candidacy if it is well designed and executed. Because of the hectic pace an abbreviated session requires, it will be much more exhausting for the pastor, search committee, deacons, and staff. Plan in advance and communicate to your congregation and the pastor what the general itinerary is. Planning the itinerary can actually take place during the time you are searching and waiting for the Lord to lead you to a man. It is helpful if the committee has shared in one of its previous monthly congregational updates a general overview of the candidacy phase. Again, remind the congregation just prior to the candidacy week what the overall schedule of events will be. Include when the special business meeting will be to determine whether a call will be extended. Make sure you adhere to your constitution's language for announcing a special business meeting. For example, there may be a statement requiring the announcement of any special business meeting to be made in two or more regular services prior to the meeting. If you abide by whatever your constitution says, there should be no major surprises for anyone during that important week. A sample itinerary has been provided in Appendix J. Your situation will demand a unique itinerary designed just for your church, but look for common characteristics that may be applicable in your situation. Copies of the itinerary should be made available for all of those directly involved, including the deacons. Here are a few tips for a successful week.

- The search committee has probably listened to a number of preaching tapes that the pastor has made available. Make copies available to the congregation several weeks in advance of the candidacy week. This may diminish a potential congregational concern of having too few opportunities to hear the man preach.

- Create a bulletin insert for candidacy Sunday. This should be a brief, one-page, résumé of the candidate. At the top should be his name and a picture. He may prefer the photo to include his wife and any children still at home. From the candidate profile he has submitted, highlight the most valuable information. Maybe a short quote from a reference known and respected by the congregation would be appropriate.

- Make sure the candidate and his family are introduced in the first service they attend. The wife will play an important part in this candidacy. If they have children, it will be good for them to interact with children within your church. If the children are teenagers, this may be a difficult time for them to be uprooted, and you should provide opportunities that will diminish apprehension on their part. Years ago I heard a man say, "Children are a man's testimony." The family, not just the man, needs to be seen during the candidating process.

- Resist any urge to assist in drafting the candidate's messages. That should be your standard practice anyway. Who are the sheep to dictate to the shepherd? Before he comes, encourage him to seek the mind of the Lord regarding message content. When the Holy Spirit works as a result of the preaching of the Word, you can confidently say that it was He alone. The committee has played no part.

- If hotel accommodations are needed, provide nice but modest accommodations for the candidate and his wife. A hotel stay will afford them a much needed private respite. It would be a nice gesture to provide a fruit basket for their room.

- See that he incurs no business expense during his stay. All travel expenses should be paid for by your church. While he is candidating, provide him with a car. It need not be a rental. Maybe someone in your church has a nice vehicle that can be spared for a few days. The candidate will want to take his wife on some drives to see the surrounding area and look at opportunities for housing. If anyone representing the church takes the candidate and his wife out to eat, make sure the church (not the candidate) picks up the tab. There may be times when he and his wife eat on their own. Ask him to turn in all receipts for reimbursement.

- Make sure you build into the hectic schedule time for him and his wife to be alone. They too will need rest and a time to freshen up between sessions.

- It would be good for your committee to create a time when the congregation can ask questions of the candidate. An excellent time for this to happen is an hour and fifteen minutes prior to the Sunday evening service. This will be a good opportunity for the congregation to hear the pastor speak on issues that may concern them. Having this meeting right before the evening service provides nice closure to this segment of the process. The next service must start on time, and the pastor needs time to begin to focus on his evening message. Finish the question-and-answer session no later than fifteen minutes prior to the next service. Determine in advance whether he wants to take questions from the floor or would rather have questions submitted for his review in advance. In this case the questions could be submitted to committeemen after the morning service. Either way is legitimate. Some candidates may feel that they have answered every conceivable question getting to that point and would rather think on their feet before the congregation. Others would like the opportunity to look over the questions, assuring an adequate response. Irrespective of which way the candidate chooses, the congregation needs to be aware that a "filter" is in place. There needs to be a standard of appropriateness communicated to the congregation. Either the search committee chairman or an assistant pastor should moderate the question-and-answer time. If the pastor chooses to take the questions from the floor, the moderator will keep a low profile. He can open and close the session and intervene in the case of an inappropriate question or for the purpose of clarifying a point. If the candidate has foreknowledge of the questions, the moderator will read the questions to him and will ask him to clarify or expand an answer when needed. The congregation needs to be aware that this is a time to hear the thoughts of the man that may become their next pastor. The motive here is not to trick, confuse, or embarrass this man of God. This time is primarily for the benefit of the congregation. The committeemen, staff, and deacons have had opportunities for their questions to be answered in other forums. They should remain fairly silent.

- Arrange for a time the candidate and his wife can socialize with other pastoral staff and their wives. This may need to be no more than a luncheon.

- If time permits, arrange for a social at a deacon's house for the candidate and his wife to meet informally with the deacons and their wives. A potluck meal will reduce the workload on any single deacon family. This meeting should have a relaxed atmosphere. Provide a brief time the ladies can be with the candidate's wife and the men can visit with the pastor. This can be a genuine time of encouragement for all in attendance.

- Have a time of prayer in the pastor's office prior to each service. Invite the deacons and staff to participate. Ask the Lord to empower the pastor to deliver the message that He has laid on his heart. Pray for the listeners as well.

- At the culmination of all of the candidacy activities, see the candidate off. Meet him and his wife at the airport or bid them farewell from the hotel if they are driving back to their home. It is a nice gesture to let him know that you will call once he has had time to settle in at home.

- When a follow-up call is made, again express your appreciation for his willingness to go through this demanding process. Unquestionably, your conversation will gravitate towards seeking each other's perspective on how the visit went. Following your special business meeting, if possible, plan a conference call to share with the pastor the vote of the people. Know which telephone number he would like you to call. Some may prefer a call at home.

The purpose of orchestrating this elaborate and intricate process of candidating is simply to ascertain the will of God. Countless questions have been asked both of the candidate and representatives of the church. Hours, days, weeks, and months have gone into finding a pastor. The corporate body has yet to speak. A great sense of anticipation begins to build as you convene your special business meeting and the vote is taken. All that can be said at this point is "May God's will be done."

12

THE CALL

And I will give you pastors according to mine heart, which shall feed you with knowledge and understanding. Jeremiah 3:15

While service is not the preliminary call, a personal relationship with the Lord is. Understanding that, there are numerous biblical references of additional callings to special ministries. "As they ministered to the Lord, and fasted, the Holy Ghost said, Separate me Barnabas and Saul for the work whereunto I have called them" (Acts 13:2). We have many examples of men chosen for service by God: Moses (Exodus 3 and 4), Samuel (I Samuel 3), Gideon (Judges 6:11-16), the twelve apostles (Mark 3:13-19), and Paul (Acts 9: 4-6).

"Called" is a term that many Christians use today to describe the process by which a person is chosen by God for a particular vocation or a particular position. Paul writes to Timothy, "Who hath saved us, and called us with an holy calling, not according to our works, but according to his own purpose and grace, which was given us in Christ Jesus before the world began" (II Timothy 1:9). The task for your search committee is to find a man that knows he has been called to this specific ministry. The man placed before your congregation has given evidence and testimony that he has been called to be a pastor. While not an apostle, the pastor you are considering should be able to say along with Paul

- "Whereof I was made a minister, according to the gift of the grace of God given unto me by the effectual working of his power" (Ephesians 3:7).

- "Whereof I am made a minister, according to the dispensation of God which is given to me for you, to fulfil the word of God" (Colossians 1:25).

- "Whereunto I am appointed a preacher, and an apostle, and a teacher of the Gentiles" (II Timothy 1:11).

- "Whereunto I am ordained a preacher, and an apostle, (I speak the truth in Christ, and lie not;) a teacher of the Gentiles in faith and verity" (I Timothy 2:7).

Basic summary of criteria for a call:

- *Given:* He is a godly man that recognizes his calling.
- *Given:* He meets the biblical standards for a pastor.
- *Given:* He has made himself available to pastor your congregation.
- *Yet to be determined:* Has he been called to your church?

Even prior to the man candidating, it would be beneficial (at a minimum) to have a Wednesday evening message or Sunday school lesson devoted to the topic of "being called." The congregation should understand that they too are "called" and have an equal obligation to be Holy Spirit led. That will be the only way for them to accurately determine the will of God in the matter of calling this man to be their pastor. "Wherefore, holy brethren, partakers of the heavenly calling, consider the Apostle and High Priest of our profession, Christ Jesus" (Hebrews 3:1). Typically in independent churches the decision to invite a man to pastor their church ultimately rests in the voice of the congregation. The deacons and the search committee are only agents of the local church. The deacons act on behalf of the congregation until the congregation itself can meet to conduct business. The congregation makes the final determination regarding issues such as calling a pastor.

The business meeting called for the purpose of voting on the candidate should be conducted as soon as possible after the candidating period is over. The meeting should be well planned. It will be helpful if the deacons work in conjunction with any pastors on staff. Following the candidate's last day with your church, the week's schedule of events can include the following:

1. The search committee (or the committee chairman and/or the deacon chairman) should meet with all assistant pastors to see if they are still confident that this man is God's man for your church. It is desirable that the assistant pastors be unanimous in their belief that the candidate is God's man for your church.

2. Conduct a short deacons' meeting prior to the special business meeting. The purpose of this meeting will be to share with the men the mind of the assistant pastors and give any feedback you may have from the candidate himself. Address any questions or concerns the deacons may have as a result of the candidacy week. The deacon chairman needs to be able to stand before the congregation and share that the deacons are united in their belief that the candidate is to be their next pastor. If this cannot be done, begin to anticipate problems that may arise during your special business meeting. If you have a split board of deacons, the probability of securing this candidate as your next pastor declines proportionately.

3. Establish in advance the order of the special business meeting. Make certain that all participants know what role they are to play. Before the business meeting one deacon should agree to make the motion when that is appropriate. You may want to have the search committee chairman make the motion and then receive a second from the floor. Your meeting should be well ordered, efficient, timely, and one that encourages dialogue. You may want to remind those in attendance, "Let all things be done decently and in order" (I Corinthians 14:40).

4. Along with the announcement that a special business meeting is being called, there should be a reminder that only members are to participate in that meeting. You may choose to allow others to attend, but they should not be allowed to participate. They are to be observers only. Some may think it unkind not to allow nonmembers even the opportunity to ask questions or make a brief comment. Remember this is the solemn business of the local church. Nonmembers (for whatever reason) are not an official part of this assembly. Certain rights and privileges need to accompany church membership, and voting on your pastor should be of the highest order.

5. While there are different meeting formats that can be employed, the following has been successfully used. After the special business meeting has been called into session with prayer, immediately have a brief question-and-answer time. An assistant pastor or the search committee chairman can chair this portion of the meeting. If an assistant pastor moderates, it is good to have the search committee chairman and the deacon chairman up front. They can take turns addressing congregational questions. This format rightfully implies to the congregation that the leadership of the church is of one mind. Allow a reasonable amount of time for dialogue.

6. After the questions are answered, the deacon chairman becomes the meeting chairman. He shares that the deacons (in agreement with the pastoral staff) believe that an invitation should be extended to the candidate to become the next pastor. The floor is open for a nomination and a second. It is best to use written, or secret, ballots. They will more accurately reveal the wishes of the people. A ballot may look similar to this and should include only a yes or no option.

> After prayer and consultation and based upon the recommendation of the pastoral search committee, an invitation should be extended to Pastor _____ to become our next senior pastor at Your Church.
>
> Yes ☐
>
> No ☐

7. Unless your constitution states differently, no absentee ballots should be allowed. While there is almost always a legitimate request made, it opens the door to a real quandary. It is unfortunate if a person cannot be a part of the special business meeting, but being in attendance that night should be a requisite to vote. Leadership does not want to take on the extra burden of determining who might be at home sick, at work, in the hospital, on vacation, or just too busy to come to the meeting. Allowing any absentee ballot to be cast will also set a precedent for future business meetings. In addition, it can place into question the validity of the vote.

8. Prearranged tellers (all members of the deacon board) should pass the ballots out to all eligible voters. Remember to offer a ballot to any eligible voter in attendance who is in some other part of the service (e.g., the nursery). The votes are cast and then collected. The deacon chairman should thank the congregation for their assistance and inform them that the results of their vote will be announced Sunday morning. The meeting is closed in prayer.

9. The tellers should go to the pastor's office, soon to be joined by the deacon chairman. The votes are tallied and rechecked for accuracy. Percentages are calculated based upon the number of ballots cast. Once counted, the ballots and the tally sheets should be kept on file for a reasonable amount of time in case the results are questioned. Your only option to prevent the possibility of a tremendous problem is to save the ballots.

10. You are now ready to place the call to the candidate at the prearranged time and designated number. It is best if the vote tabulation has exceeded the constitutional minimum requirement and has met the minimum percentage the pastor may have set for himself. If he has ever shared with the committee a percentage that he would expect in order to accept a call, keep those numbers private within the committee. When you call the pastor to disclose the results of the vote, you may also choose to share the general tenor of the meeting with him.

11. If the vote numbers are favorable and the pastor accepts the call, you have a pastor! Take time to rejoice together. Discuss briefly details such as signing contracts and when he plans to join you. Tell the pastor that you will be announcing the results of the vote and his response in the next Sunday morning service. Express your desire for him to keep the results private within his family until Sunday. It is nice if both congregations can be informed at the same time, negating the impact of rumors. Your deacon chairman should stand before the congregation to share with them the results of their vote and the positive reply of the candidate. Inform them briefly of the time line for his arrival.

12. If the vote is not favorable, do not be disheartened. Trust that God has spoken through your congregation and proceed with your search. Encourage the candidate, your congregation, and yourselves that God has a man for your ministry. It may be easy for the committee to

become disheartened and discouraged. Should this happen, those attitudes will be seen by the congregation and will have a negative impact upon the congregation. God is still on His throne and willing to underwrite this undertaking.

The congregation is now ready to begin making plans for one of the most exciting times in a church's history: the arrival of their new pastor!

13

TRANSITION—THE FIRST YEAR

But he that glorieth, let him glory in the Lord.
II Corinthians 10:17

Fantastic, you have a pastor! Even though he may not be on the scene yet, the thought of his coming is exhilarating and has breathed new life into your camp. The spirit of expectation has lifted the hearts of your people. They are eager for the new pastor and his family to arrive. There are only a few tasks left to be done that will facilitate a smooth transition. The Lord has removed the weight of finding a pastor from the committeemen. Some members of your congregation will want to express their appreciation for a job well done by your committee. Accept their words of appreciation, but do not forget to point to the one who has led all the way. Remember Paul's admonition after quieting his opponents. We are not to boast of man's abilities but rather God's (I Corinthians 3:21). Paul earlier reminded the Corinthians of the same principle in I Corinthians 1:31, "He that glorieth, let him glory in the Lord." The committee, after having gone through such a spiritually demanding and personally refining endeavor, will want to give their Lord all the credit.

Search committee, it is time to focus your attention on a few details that can be easily overlooked in the excitement of the hour. The emphasis of finding a pastor is beginning to shift toward taking care of your pastor. There begins to be a subtle transfer in leadership responsibilities from the committee chairman back to the deacon chairman.

Addressing any of the following details will certainly be an encouragement to your new pastor and his family.

Before the Pastor Arrives

1. If the pastor lives nearby and if he and your committee can meet, do so and secure a signed contract. Have an original copy for the pastor and an original copy for the church as well. Record that document with your church secretary. If the pastor is unavailable to meet, take care of this business through overnight mail.

2. Once a contract has been signed, the official duties of the search committee cease. The secretary should contact all pastors that remain in your "candidate pool." He should express the committee's appreciation to those pastors for their willingness to be a part of this process. The secretary's final act should be to send a letter of appreciation to all individuals that played a key role in giving your committee guidance. Copies of those letters are given to the deacon chairman for the record. The secretary can now be excused from duty. The deacon chairman should collect the notebooks from each of the committeemen. It is wise to retain a single copy for the historical records of your church. In such a case, **eliminate *all* information on *all* candidates considered** with the exception of your new pastor. *In addition, make sure his financial statement has been expunged from the record.* Destroy all other contents of all of the notebooks. Place this document along with your Church Profile into your church archives.

3. Most pastors cannot immediately drop what they are doing and come to your church. There may be a period of several weeks (or longer) before your new pastor can actually join you. During this time his efforts will be twofold: (1) closing out his previous ministry, and (2) focusing his attention on his new ministry. You will want the transition to be as smooth and as quick as possible. If the pastor is moving from another church to yours without interruption, make sure he is never without a paycheck. This may mean that he will be on your church's payroll *before* his first official Sunday, *but not before* a contract is signed. Compensating the pastor for more than one month of transitional salary is atypical. If the pastor desires to take his family on a vacation, your church is under no obligation to underwrite his salary during the

vacation. Only when his attention has turned to your congregation are you obliged.

4. Raise the question of health insurance with your new pastor. Address any needs he may have regarding insurance. Make sure that his family's health insurance does not expire between ministries and thereby leave him and his family without coverage. Offer to reimburse him for all out of pocket expenditures related to health care coverage until he is on your church plan. Work with your church treasurer to expedite the paperwork.

5. Remind the pastor that his moving expenses will be paid for by your church. The deacon chairman should personally monitor this part of the transition. Payment can be made directly to the moving company or the pastor.

6. Discuss with the new pastor the possibility of having an installation service. Many pastors like to designate a specific Sunday service for this purpose. It should be a dedicatory service both for the pastor and the congregation. He may want to invite a friend or colleague to speak at such a service. Because of conflicting schedules, an installation service is usually not the first Sunday a pastor is in your church, but it does typically take place in the first month. An installation service is an official way of declaring that a new chapter in your church's history is being written. Again, pay for all expenses for travel, housing, and accommodations of your guests. After the installation service, it is nice to provide refreshments in the fellowship hall.

7. Any stationery, tracts, pens, or bulletins used by the church should be reprinted to include the new pastor's name. Buy only about a month's supply of stationery and bulletins because the new pastor may want to change their format. The question is always raised about what to do with the outdated materials. If you wrestle with not wanting to dispose of stationery and tracts, realize the prudence of making a definitive break between ministries. The benefit of trying to save a few dollars may be quickly outweighed by causing others to revisit the past. If asked, most pastors would prefer any documents (or tools) used by the church to reflect the current ministerial staff. Start fresh!

8. Make any changes necessary to the pastor's church office that will make his work environment more professional, useful, and inviting.

9. Almost every church has a sign or message board in front of their church building. Many of those signs include the pastor's name along with times of service. The last pastor's name may have been removed months ago. Make sure the new pastor's name is in place before his arrival.

10. If the house the pastor is going to be moving into is his, there may be a number of things that the members can do to be of assistance. Help with mowing grass, trimming shrubs, painting interior and exterior, refurbishing rooms, and tearing out old and installing new carpet. Make sure all of the work has been preapproved with the pastor, especially when it comes to paint and other color schemes.

11. The search committee chairman and/or the deacon chairman should plan a time to sit down with the interim pastor. On behalf of the committee and the congregation, express your appreciation for a job well done. Comment specifically on how the Lord has used him to fill a most difficult position. Discreetly remind him that his current rate of pay will revert to his regular level of compensation once the new pastor arrives. In an effort to have no misunderstanding, you might want to agree upon the day his rate of pay will change. Communicate that agreement to the person in charge of payroll in your church.

When the Pastor Arrives

1. Have church members assist in unloading any moving vans the pastor has rented. If a commercial line is used, allow them to do their work and be available to help the pastor after the commercial movers leave. Several ladies of the church can be especially helpful in assisting the pastor's wife with some of the finer details of moving into the new residence.

2. Some church congregations like to have a "food shower" for the pastor's family. After several weeks of collecting foodstuffs at church (before their arrival), the goods can be officially delivered by a couple of the deacons' wives. Some churches choose to have a churchwide reception at which time the household goods are presented.

3. Prearrange with the pastor that he, his wife, and any family members are to come forward for membership at the end of the first Sunday morning service. The format followed may be slightly different from

normal procedures. The candidates for membership have already been thoroughly investigated regarding their salvation, baptism, and so forth. On the other hand, you don't want to give the impression that they became members by default. Have them come forward after the message to stand before the congregation. Either an assistant pastor or the deacon chairman can preside over this formality and can ask for the vote of the congregation. Keep this simple and quick.

4. Suggest to the pastor that he officially recognize the ability and efforts of your interim pastor for the work he has done during the interim. At the very least, the new pastor should publicly acknowledge the interim pastor. A plaque is a simple but lasting reminder of a job well done. Some new pastors have chosen to give the interim a few days with his wife and family on a mini-vacation. Keep in mind the interim pastor will have a significant block of folks that truly appreciate the job he has done. When the new pastor acknowledges the interim's efforts, the new pastor begins to build a bond between himself, the interim pastor, and the congregation.

To the Deacon Chairman and Deacons

You have undoubtedly grown close to the pastor over the past few weeks and months. You have seen God answer your prayers by supplying your congregation with His choice. You and your wives have socialized with the new pastor and his wife and have become really good friends. Continue to foster your relationship with him on two fronts. To some individuals these two fronts may appear to be diametrically opposed, but I believe them to be congruent.

First, as he allows, *grow even closer to your pastor.*

• Establish a relationship in which the pastor can share his goals, needs, hopes, desires, and misgivings without fear of reprisal or breach of confidentiality. One errant philosophy within the field of ministry teaches that pastors should establish no genuinely close relationships with anyone in their congregation. In such cases pastors that are hurting often confide in others around the country. Following this idea eliminates the opportunity for a deacon, or a congregation, to assist their pastor. Outside counsel is at times helpful, but the pastor and the deacon chairman have the responsibility of developing an honest and open relationship between each other.

- Help your pastor understand people and programs within your church.
- Suggest courses of action and warn him of apparent pitfalls. Do not require that your suggestions be implemented. Listen to him. Allow him to lead.
- Assist him as he prepares for his first business meeting.
- Look for ways to be an encouragement to him and his family.
- If he is spending too much time in the office, persuade him to take time off from work and spend time with his wife and family.
- Pray for *and with* your pastor on a regular basis. Meet to pray with him, in his office, before he delivers a message from the pulpit. Invite others to be a part of this time of prayer. This is a great way for even young Christians to get to know their pastor.

Second, *allow others to be able to get close to your pastor.* During the first few months of his service you may need to organize some social or business contacts.

- It is important that you introduce the pastor and his wife to other couples within the congregation.
- Allow the pastor to gravitate towards those folks that have similar interests. If he likes to golf, get him with golfers. If he likes to fish or hunt, pair him with people with similar interests.
- Introduce your pastor to the local banker in charge of your church accounts and to township personnel such as the supervisor or building inspector. These kinds of contacts may prove to be beneficial.
- Do not forget about his wife. Ask the pastor often how she is doing. She may be overwhelmed trying to acclimate to a new home, church, friends, schedule, and possibly even a different climate. Work with the pastor to see that her needs are met.

While the pastor develops other relationships within the congregation, it will become necessary for the deacon chairman to begin to play a lesser role. Allow other members to get to know their pastor. Do not become jealous of your pastor. Learn to share him with others. Finally, it seems to be human nature for us to give a lot of attention to something (or someone) new. Likewise, it is just as natural for us to overlook that which has become commonplace. Especially during the first year you should be aware of your pastor and his family's needs. Take advantage of every opportunity to be his champion.

May you serve the Lord together in grace and peace. "Beloved, I wish above all things that thou mayest prosper and be in health, even as thy soul prospereth" (III John 2).

EPILOGUE

What a journey this has been. It may have started with the question "Why?" but ended with the acclamation "Why not, my Lord?" Issues seemingly too painful to confront turned into perseverance to do right. "Why me?" surrendered to "Is there not a cause?" When buffeted, you found safe harbor. Through the direction of the Holy Spirit "self" was replaced by corporate effort. That in turn was further refined, under His direction, until only His will mattered. The focus of "our ministry" dramatically shifted to "His ministry." Confusion was transformed into determined resolve. A threatened congregation soon rallied behind its leaders. Questions received answers. Question marks were replaced with exclamation points. Christians with shallow prayer lives were driven to new depths. Answered prayers were required, expected, and obtained. Faith was stretched. Strength to go on was bolstered by our Comforter. Doors of opportunity opened. One by one they closed until there was only one door left through which to pass. Tears that revealed broken hearts were replaced with tears of joy. Satan had taken his best shot at disheveling a ministry. His attempt was thwarted by the one who died for this church. Assurance in man was replaced with an unshakable reliance on God.

You set out on a journey *In Search of God's Man* and you found him! Having trusted solely in the Lord, this journey has made you only more fit for the Master's use. To God be the glory!

"Ye are of God, little children, and have overcome them: because greater is he that is in you, than he that is in the world" (I John 4:4).

APPENDICES

APPENDIX A

YOUR CHURCH

PASTORAL SEARCH COMMITTEE

Trust in the Lord with all thine heart; and lean not unto thine own understanding. In all thy ways acknowledge him, and he shall direct thy paths. Proverbs 3:5-6

APPENDIX B

Possible Pastoral Credentials

For Meeting: ——————
Date

A man that

- loves the Lord and is an example of His holiness

- believes in the autonomy and independent nature of the local fundamentalist church

- knows he has been called to preach and loves carrying out that call

- loves prayer, recognizes its benefits, exercises the privilege, and is a model for his deacons and congregation

- loves missions and soulwinning

- understands the need for personal and professional accountability and has established that in his current ministry

- has experience in operating a Christian school

- has good "business sense," including a working knowledge of a viable budget, and has experience in a building program

- believes that weekly prayer meetings are important

- is available to, and communicates with, his staff and the local church members and keeps regular office hours

- loves to pastor his flock and looks at his ministry as more than a job

APPENDIX C

CHURCH LETTERHEAD
Date
Contact's Name
Church and/or Street Address
City, State, Zip

Dear Contact's Name:
As you may be aware, our senior pastor here at Your Church recently tendered his resignation. As a deacon board we regretfully accepted his resignation and have started the process of searching for God's man for this ministry. Our search committee has begun to correspond with a few men that personally know this ministry. We were wondering if you would be able to recommend someone who might be uniquely qualified to become our senior pastor.

To assist you in your prayerful consideration, we have listed a few characteristics that we consider desirable attributes in a pastor.

WALKS WITH THE LORD WITH ALL HIS HEART, SOUL, AND MIND
(1) Strong preacher
(2) Ministers to and serves his flock
(3) Evangelistic and missionary minded
(4) Mature in character and ministry
(5) Committed to excellence in Christian education

If you believe that you can be of assistance, please contact me either by mail or by phone:

Name
Street Address
City, State, Zip

Phone number:
E-mail:

Yours in Christ,

Signature

Name
Pastoral Search Committee Secretary
Chairman of the Deacon Board

APPENDIX D

Date
Candidate's Name
Street Address
City, State, Zip

Dear Pastor ⸺⸺⸺⸺:
I received your letter stating your interest in the vacant pastoral position here at Your Church. I have given your letter to the Pastoral Search Committee for their perusal. Should they have any further questions, I assure you they will get in touch with you.

I want to personally thank you for taking the time and showing an interest in God's ministry here at Your Church. We covet your prayers as we seek God's will in determining His choice in this matter.

In His Service,

Signature

Name
Pastoral Search Committee Secretary
Chairman of the Deacon Board

APPENDIX E

Seventeen Requirements for the Pastor According to Titus 1:6-9

Titus 1:6

1. Blameless in community
2. The husband of one wife
3. Faithful children who are not riotous or unruly

Titus 1:7

4. Blameless as a bishop
5. Not self-willed
6. Not soon angry
7. Not given to wine
8. No striker
9. Not given to filthy lucre

Titus 1:8

10. Lover of hospitality
11. Lover of good men
12. Sober
13. Just
14. Holy
15. Temperate

Titus 1:9

16. Holds fast to the faithful word as he has been taught
17. Able by sound doctrine to exhort and convince the gainsayers

Titus 1:6-9

If any be blameless, the husband of one wife, having faithful children not accused of riot or unruly. [7] For a bishop must be blameless, as the steward of God; not selfwilled, not soon angry, not given to wine, no striker, not given to filthy lucre; [8] but a lover of hospitality, a lover of good men, sober, just, holy, temperate; [9] holding fast the faithful word as he hath been taught, that he may be able by sound doctrine both to exhort and to convince the gainsayers.

NINETEEN REQUIREMENTS FOR THE PASTOR ACCORDING TO I TIMOTHY 3:1-7

I TIMOTHY 3:1

1. Desires the office

I TIMOTHY 3:2

2. Blameless
3. The husband of one wife
4. Vigilant
5. Sober
6. Of good behavior
7. Given to hospitality
8. Apt to teach

I TIMOTHY 3:3

9. Not given to wine
10. Not a striker
11. Not greedy
12. Patient
13. Not a brawler
14. Not covetous

I TIMOTHY 3:4

15. Rules his own house well
16. Children in subjection

I TIMOTHY 3:6

17. Not a novice
18. Without pride

I TIMOTHY 3:7

19. Good report

I TIMOTHY 3:1-7

This is a true saying, If a man desire the office of a bishop, he desireth a good work. [2] A bishop then must be blameless, the husband of one wife, vigilant, sober, of good behaviour, given to hospitality, apt to teach; [3] not given to wine, no striker, not greedy of filthy lucre; but patient, not a brawler, not covetous; [4] one that ruleth well his own house, having his children in subjection with all gravity; [5] (for if a man know not how to rule his own house, how shall he take care of the church of God?) [6] not a novice, lest being lifted up with pride he fall into the condemnation of the devil. [7] Moreover he must have a good report of them which are without; lest he fall into reproach and the snare of the devil.

CHARACTERISTICS OF THE PASTORS

Called by God—Exod. 28:1; Heb. 5:4

Qualified by God—Isa. 6:5-7; II Cor. 3:5-6

Commissioned by Christ—Matt. 28:19

Sent by the Holy Spirit—Acts 13:2, 4

Separated to the gospel—Rom. 1:1

Have authority from God—II Cor. 10:8; 13:10

That authority is for edification—II Cor. 10:8; 13:10

Entrusted with the gospel—I Thess. 2:4

Pastors are described as

Ambassadors for Christ—II Cor. 5:20

Ministers of Christ—I Cor. 4:1

Stewards of the mysteries of God—I Cor. 4:1

Defenders of the faith—Phil. 1:17

The servants of Christ's people—II Cor. 4:5

Specially provided by God—Rom. 10:14-15

Laboring in vain without God's blessing—I Cor. 3:7; 15:10

Compared to earthen vessels—II Cor. 4:7

Pastors should be

Pure—Isa. 52:11; I Tim. 3:9

Holy—Exod. 28:36; Lev. 21:6; Titus 1:8

Humble—Acts 20:19

Patient—II Cor. 6:4; II Tim. 2:24

Blameless—I Tim. 3:2; Titus 1:7

Willing—Isa. 6:8; I Pet. 5:2

Disinterested—II Cor. 12:14; I Thess. 2:6

Impartial—I Tim. 5:21

Gentle—I Thess. 2:7; II Tim. 2:24

Devoted—Acts 20:24; Phil. 1:20-21

Strong in grace—II Tim. 2:1

Self-denying—I Cor. 9:27

Sober, just, and temperate—Titus 1:8

Hospitable—I Tim. 3:2; Titus 1:8

Apt to teach—I Tim. 3:2; II Tim. 2:24

Studious and meditative—I Tim. 4:13, 15

Watchful—II Tim. 4:5

Prayerful—Eph. 3:14; Phil. 1:4

Strict in ruling their own families—I Tim. 3:4

Affectionate to their people—Phil. 1:7; I Thess. 2:8, 11

Example to the flock—Phil. 3:17; II Thess. 3:9; I Tim. 4:12,
I Pet. 5:3

Pastors should

Seek the salvation of their flock—I Cor. 10:33

Avoid giving unnecessary offence—I Cor. 10:32-33; II Cor. 6:3;
Rom. 14:13

Make full proof of their ministry—II Tim. 4:5

Pastors should not be

Lords over God's heritage—I Pet. 5:3

Greedy of filthy lucre—Acts 20:33; I Tim. 3:3; I Pet. 5:2

Contentious—I Tim. 3:3; Titus 1:7

Crafty—II Cor. 4:2

Men-pleasers—Gal. 1:10; I Thess. 2:4

Easily dispirited—II Cor. 4:8-9; 6:10

Entangled by cares—Luke 9:60; II Tim. 2:4

Given to wine—I Tim. 3:3; Titus 1:7

Pastors are bound to

Preach the gospel to all—Mark 16:15; I Cor. 1:17

Feed the church—Jer. 3:15; John 21:15-17; Acts 20:28; I Pet. 5:2

Build up the church—II Cor. 12:19; Eph. 4:12

Watch for souls—Heb. 13:17

Pray for their people—Joel 2:17; Col. 1:9

Strengthen the faith of their people—Luke 22:32; Acts 14:22

Teach—II Tim. 2:2

Exhort—Titus 1:9; 2:15

Warn affectionately—Acts 20:31

Rebuke—Titus 1:13; 2:15

Comfort—II Cor. 1:4-6

Convince gainsayers—Titus 1:9

War a good warfare—I Tim. 1:18; II Tim. 4:7

Endure hardness—II Tim. 2:3

Pastors should preach

Christ crucified—Acts 8:5, 35; I Cor. 2:2

Repentance and faith—Acts 20:21

According to the oracles of God—I Pet. 4:11

Everywhere—Mark 16:20; Acts 8:4

Not with enticing words of man's wisdom—I Cor. 1:17; 2:1, 4

Not setting forth themselves—II Cor. 4:5

Without deceitfulness—II Cor. 2:17; 4:2; I Thess. 2:3, 5

Fully, and without reserve—Acts 5:20; 20:20, 27; Rom. 15:19

With boldness—Isa. 58:1; Ezek. 2:6; Matt. 10:27-28

With plainness of speech—II Cor. 3:12

With zeal—I Thess. 2:8

With constancy—Acts 6:4; II Tim. 4:2

With consistency—II Cor. 1:18-19

With heedfulness—I Tim. 4:16

With good will and love—Phil. 1:15-17

With faithfulness—Ezek. 3:17-18

Without charge, if possible—I Cor. 9:18; I Thess. 2:9

Woe to those who do not preach the gospel—I Cor. 9:16

When faithful, pastors

Approve themselves as the ministers of God—II Cor. 6:4

Thank God for His gifts to their people—I Cor. 1:4; Phil. 1:3;
I Thess. 3:9
Glory in their people—II Cor. 7:4
Rejoice in the faith and holiness of their people—I Thess. 3:6-9
Commend themselves to the consciences of men—II Cor. 4:2
Are rewarded—Matt. 24:47; I Cor. 3:14; 9:17-18; I Pet. 5:4

When unfaithful, pastors
Are spiritually insensitive—Isa. 56:10-12; Titus 1:10-11
Deal treacherously with their people—John 10:12
Delude men—Jer. 6:14; Matt. 15:14; Titus 1:10-11
Seek gain—Isa. 56:10-12; Mic. 3:11; II Pet. 2:3
Shall be punished—Ezek. 33:6-8; Matt. 24:48-51

Their people are bound to
Regard them as God's messengers—I Cor. 4:1; Gal. 4:14
Help them—Rom. 16:9; Phil. 4:3
Not despise them—Luke 10:16; I Tim. 4:12
Attend to their instructions—Mal. 2:7; Matt. 23:3
Follow their holy example—I Cor. 11:1; Phil. 3:17
Imitate their faith—Heb. 13:7
Hold them in reputation—Phil. 2:29; I Thess. 5:13; I Tim. 5:17
Love them—II Cor. 8:7; I Thess. 3:6
Pray for them—Rom. 15:30; II Cor. 1:11; Eph. 6:19; Heb. 13:18
Obey them—I Cor. 16:16; Heb. 13:17
Give them joy—II Cor. 1:14; 2:3
Support them—II Chron. 31:4; I Cor. 9:7-11; Gal. 6:6
Pray for the increase of—Matt. 9:38

Pastoral Search Committee Ministerial Lesson

Date:

Lesson presented by

A minister is bound to

I. Feed the church.

(Jer. 3:15) "And I will give you pastors according to mine heart, which shall feed you with knowledge and understanding."

(John 21:15-17) "So when they had dined, Jesus saith to Simon Peter, Simon, *son* of Jonas, lovest thou me more than these? He saith unto him, Yea, Lord; thou knowest that I love thee. He saith unto him, Feed my lambs. [16] He saith to him again the second time, Simon, *son* of Jonas, lovest thou me? He saith unto him, Yea, Lord; thou knowest that I love thee. He saith unto him, Feed my sheep. [17] He saith unto him the third time, Simon, *son* of Jonas, lovest thou me? Peter was grieved because he said unto him the third time, Lovest thou me? And he said unto him, Lord, thou knowest all things; thou knowest that I love thee. Jesus saith unto him, Feed my sheep."

(Acts 20:28) "Take heed therefore unto yourselves, and to all the flock, over the which the Holy Ghost hath made you overseers, to feed the church of God, which he hath purchased with his own blood."

(I Pet. 5:2) "Feed the flock of God which is among you, taking the oversight thereof, not by constraint, but willingly; not for filthy lucre, but of a ready mind."

• He is to feed the flock.

• He is to oversee through personal care and vigilance.

• He is not to use constraint: compulsion, tyranny, or coercive force.

• He is to be an example in _____, _____.

• He is not to lord over God's _____.

"The best way a minister can take to engage the respect of a people is to discharge his own duty among them in the best manner he can and to be a constant example to them of all that is good."

II. Build up the church.

(II Cor. 12:19) "Again, think ye that we excuse ourselves unto you? we speak before God in Christ: but *we do* all things, dearly beloved, for your edifying."

(Eph. 4:12) "For the perfecting of the saints, for the work of the ministry, for the edifying of the body of Christ."

"Perfecting": Bringing into an _____ spiritual state—members once _____ by sin.

"Working": Members harmoniously working for the good of the _____.

"Edifying": Building up the church _____ and _____ growth.

III. Watch for souls.

(Heb. 13:17) "Obey them that have the rule over you, and submit yourselves: for they watch for your souls, as they that must give account, that they may do it with joy, and not with grief: for that is unprofitable for you."

Obedience: Not blind submission but in the light of God's Word.

Giving an account: They will be found _____ or _____.

No authority to lord over but to _____.

If a faithful minister is not successful, the _____ will be his, but the _____ will be the people's.

IV. Pray for his people.

(Joel 2:17) "Let the priests, the ministers of the LORD, weep between the porch and the altar, and let them say, Spare thy people, O LORD, and give not thine heritage to reproach, that the heathen should rule over them: wherefore should they say among the people, Where is their God?"

(Col. 1:9) "For this cause we also, since the day we heard it, do not cease to pray for you, and to desire that ye might be filled with the knowledge of his will in all wisdom and spiritual understanding."

- Our knowledge of the will of God must always be _____.

- We must know it before we can do it!

- "Wisdom" is knowing how to apply general knowledge that will yield His blessing.

Good _____ without a good _____ will not profit.

V. Strengthen the faith of his people.

(Luke 22:32) "But I have prayed for thee, that thy faith fail not: and when thou art converted, strengthen thy brethren."

(Acts 14:22) "Confirming the souls of the disciples, and exhorting them to continue in the faith, and that we must through much tribulation enter into the kingdom of God."

- Fortify the believers' resolution in the strength of Christ.

- Teach them to _____ no matter what it may cost.

The best ministers *often* encourage their flock to persevere.

- Is it not "they must" but rather "we must" endure.

This matter is fixed unalterably! I Thess. 3:3

APPENDIX F

YOUR CHURCH
PASTORAL CANDIDACY PROFILE

_____
Date

I. Personal

_____
Name

_____
Street   City   State   Zip

Social Security Number: _____/____/_____

Phone (   )_____ Birth Date ___/___/___ Age ____

Marital Status: Married ____   Single ____   Widowed ____

                    Divorced ____   Separated ____   Remarried ____

Names of family members

Wife _____ Birth date _____

Child _____ Birth date _____ Grade in school ____

Child _____ Birth date _____ Grade in school ____

Child _____ Birth date _____ Grade in school ____

Child _____ Birth date _____ Grade in school ____

Child _____ Birth date _____ Grade in school ____

Education and training

School   Address   Date of graduation   Degree

_____

_____

_____

_____

_____

Have you been ordained? ____ Where? _____When? _____

By Whom? _____

List societies, boards, and professional memberships to which you belong (and any leadership positions held).

_____

_____

_____

List any honors you have received.

_____

_____

_____

_____

_____

List employment beginning with the most recent.

Name	Address	Dates	Reason for leaving

List ministries outside the local church in which you have been involved.

_____

_____

_____

_____

Do you, or a family member, have any health limitations? If so, please describe them and any unique accommodations required to support these.

_____

_____

_____

Do you have any financial debts? If so, please list to whom and an approximate amount.

_____

_____

_____

Please return with this profile an official transcript reflecting your current credit rating.

Do you have a criminal record or past moral indiscretion? _____ If so, please write an explanation on a separate sheet of paper. This will be kept in strict confidence.

Are you willing to undergo a criminal background check? _____

How do you view the role of your wife in your ministry?

_____

_____

_____

Is your wife in agreement with your ministry?

_____

_____

How does your relationship with your wife affect your ministry?

_____

_____

_____

How does your relationship with your children affect your ministry?

_____

_____

_____

List some books you have read in the last two years that impressed you.

_____

_____

List any special talents you and your family have, such as music, children's ministries, secretarial skills.

_____

_____

_____

List three adjectives that best describe strengths of your personality.

_____

List three adjectives that best describe weaknesses of your personality.

_____

II. Spiritual

Briefly describe your personal salvation experience and your call to the ministry.

_____

_____

_____

_____

_____

Briefly describe your personal relationship with the Lord in the following areas:

Prayer/Faith/Trust _____

_____

_____

Personal devotions _____

_____

_____

Bible study _____

_____

_____

Spiritual leadership in the home _____

_____

_____

What is your primary spiritual gift? _____

List any characteristics of the other spiritual gifts that may be fairly dominant in your life.

_____

_____

_____

Is your methodology of text presentation topical, expository, or other?

_____

What version(s) of the Bible do you recommend? Which do you use and for what purpose?

_____

_____

_____

In the first column rate the importance of the capabilities that a senior pastor should have, and in the second column rate how you perceive your respective strengths.

Capability	Least Important 1 2 3 4 5 6 7 8 9 10 Very Important	
	SENIOR PASTOR	**YOU**
Administration	_____	_____
Hospitality	_____	_____
Long-range planning	_____	_____
Praying	_____	_____
Preaching	_____	_____
Soulwinning	_____	_____
Studying	_____	_____
Teaching	_____	_____

Please list those areas in which you are seeking to improve yourself (and steps you are be taking).

_____

_____

_____

III. Philosophy of Ministries

Give a brief overview of your philosophy of ministry.

_____

_____

_____

_____

What have you done to enhance the services where you presently serve?

Sunday A.M. _____

_____

Sunday P.M. _____

_____

Midweek _____

_____

Describe your philosophy of church visitation programs.

_____

_____

_____

How do you view the role of women ministering in the church?

_____

_____

_____

Describe your views on music in the church and what role the senior pastor should play in choir/hymn selections.

_____

_____

_____

Please attach the music selections in your church for the past two months.

Describe your views on Christian and secular education.

Elementary _____

_____

Secondary _____

_____

Post-secondary _____

_____

Describe your general philosophy of the senior pastor's role as it relates to a K-12 church-run school.

_____

_____

_____

Home schooling _____

_____

_____

IV. Doctrine

Please submit a copy of your doctrinal statement with this questionnaire. Please briefly include your views on at least the following: Neo-evangelicalism, Calvinism/Arminianism, humanism, New Age teaching, atonement, missions, separation, standards, spiritual gifts, and the church's involvement in politics.

What is your position regarding divorce and remarriage? What areas of service can divorced individuals have in the church? What areas of service would they be disqualified from?

_____

_____

_____

_____

_____

_____

What is your position regarding the requirements for participation in the Lord's Supper?

_____

_____

_____

What is your position regarding the present-day Charismatic movement? Promise Keepers?

_____

_____

_____

Are there any church group organizations with which you enjoy fellowshiping?

_____

_____

_____

V. Role of the Local Church

Describe your overall philosophy regarding the role of the local church.

_____

_____

_____

_____

What is your position on the interaction of your church with other Bible-believing, Bible-teaching churches?

_____

_____

_____

_____

What should be the role of the church regarding missions?

Activity	Little Involved 1 2 3 4 5 6 7 8 9 10 Very Active
Work with the mission board	_____
Pastor traveling to the field	_____
Lay members traveling to the field	_____
Interviewing missionary candidates	_____
Level of support for home-church missionaries	_____
Level of support of others	_____
Faith promise giving	_____

What is your philosophy regarding midweek services/activities?

_____

_____

_____

What role should the Sunday school play in the church? What should be its scope?

_____

_____

_____

What is the role of counseling in the local church, and what role would you play as senior pastor?

_____

_____

_____

What is your view of the role of a bus ministry?

_____

_____

_____

What is the role of the local church regarding social issues (e.g., abortion, pornography, drugs, alcohol, etc.)? List any affiliations with organizations that you have (or have had) relating to the above issues.

_____

_____

_____

_____

_____

_____

In order of priority, what are the top three activities you have used to help your church grow?

_____

_____

_____

VI. Church Government

What is your position regarding the organization and leadership of the local church?

Role of the Pastor _____

_____

_____

_____

Role of the Deacon Board _____

_____

_____

_____

Role of Staff Members _____

_____

_____

_____

Role of the Congregation _____

_____

_____

_____

VII. Administration

Prioritize the top five functions of the senior pastor and indicate the approximate percentage of time you would allocate to each function per week.

_____

_____

_____

_____

Briefly describe your leadership/managerial style.

_____

_____

_____

What are the key qualities you would desire in the following?

Youth Pastor _____

_____

_____

_____

Associate Pastor _____

_____

_____

_____

Music Director _____

_____

_____

_____

Christian School Administrator _____

_____

_____

_____

Christian School Teachers _____

_____

_____

_____

Other Staff Members _____

_____

_____

_____

Please attach a list of every special speaker (and the organization each represents) that you have had in your pulpit in the past two years. Are there any
you would not recommend having back?

VIII. Miscellaneous

Please list any other information that you feel is pertinent in helping us to
determine whether you would be God's man for Your Church.

_____

_____

_____

_____

_____

_____

_____

_____

IX. References

Please list five references we may contact who are in a position to discuss your qualifications as senior pastor for Your Church.

Name   Address   Relationship   Phone

_____

_____

_____

_____

_____

THE WIFE'S PROFILE

Briefly describe your salvation experience. (Feel free to use an additional sheet.)

_____

_____

_____

Please describe your involvement with your husband's ministry, including special talents such as music and ladies' and children's ministries.

_____

_____

_____

Please describe the ministries in which you have served or you think God would have you serve both within and outside the local church.

_____

_____

Briefly describe your personal relationship with the Lord in the following areas:

Prayer/Faith/Trust _____

_____

Personal devotions _____

_____

Bible study _____

_____

List societies, boards, and professional memberships to which you belong (and leadership positions held).

_____

_____

Do you have any issues in your life that could be a hindrance to your husband's ministry?

_____

_____

Describe how you balance your home life with that of being a pastor's wife.

_____

_____

_____

How do you feel about a pastor's wife having employment outside the church or home?

_____

_____

_____

On another sheet, please share any other pertinent information you deem valuable to our decision-making process.

APPENDIX G

CHURCH LETTERHEAD
Date
Candidate's Name
Street Address
City, State, Zip

Dear _____:

As per our telephone conversation on Wednesday, June 13, 2002, we are forwarding to you our Pastoral Candidacy Profile. We are sure that you will find it quite thorough, but it is not meant to be overwhelming. To the best of our ability, we have attempted not to be repetitive in our questions. Please be assured that sensitive information requested within the application will be kept in the strictest confidence.

Upon receipt and review of your profile, the Pastoral Search Committee will be narrowing the field of potential candidates to one. Should we have any further questions, we will contact you. In the meantime if you should have any questions for us, please feel free to give either of us a call. The committee would appreciate your returning the completed application within twenty-one days of the above date.

We thank you for your prayerful consideration,

Signature

Name
Pastoral Search Committee Chairman
Phone:
E-mail:

Signature

Name
Deacon Chairman
Phone:
E-mail:

APPENDIX H

Examples of Possible Questions for a Visit or Second Round of Questioning

(These questions should be the result of conversations to date with the potential candidate. Your questions will undoubtedly be different.)

Where do you see yourself in five years?

Why do you believe that you are God's man for Your Church?

What vision is God giving you for YC?

Please describe your current accounting/budget system for your

Church

School

Are you aware of YC's accounting system?

Is there anything you might change should you be established as our next pastor?

What checks and balances do you have built in to safeguard against accusations of misappropriations of church funds?

What additional systems do you employ to hold yourself accountable?

What kind of financial and supplemental wage package would you need if you were to become our pastor?

Would you make any changes in full-time staff upon your arrival at YC?

Does your current church encourage short-term mission trips?

Adults

Youth

Describe your wife's involvement in the ministry.

Current

Future

APPENDIX I

Questions for Reference

_____   _____
Potential Candidate   Reference

1. How long have you known _____?

2. Have you ever worked together in the ministry? How? Where? When?

3. What is _____'s greatest asset?

4. Is _____ capable of delegating duties?

5. Do you know of any situation or personal characteristic that we should be concerned about if we should consider calling _____ to candidate?

6. Do you know his wife? How does she complement his ministry?

7. Would you personally recommend _____ as a candidate?

APPENDIX J

This is an actual itinerary used during a church's pastoral search. Names have been replaced, however, with men's positions.

Candidacy Week Itinerary

Date: _____

Wednesday
- Deacons' meeting to vote on senior pastor's wage package

Friday
- Arrival of candidate and wife at the airport (approximately 10:20 A.M.)
- Pick up car and go to Comfort Inn
- Lunch: On their own
- Assistant pastor and candidate meet
- 1:00 P.M. Residential builder (member of the church) and candidate and his wife look at housing options (meet at church and go from there)
- 2:30 P.M. Meet the assistant pastor and wife at the church
- Dinner: For the candidate and his wife at a church couple's home (time will be mutually agreed upon)

Saturday
- 9:00 A.M. Breakfast at assistant deacon chairman's home (search committee chairman, the deacon chairman, and vice chairman, and their wives)
- Go over salary package, itinerary for Candidate Sunday, and any other issues needing to be addressed
- 10:30 A.M. Deacon chairman and wife meet with candidate and wife
- 11:30 A.M. Candidate/wife have lunch and the afternoon on their own
- 6:00 P.M. Deacons' Potluck Dinner Social at a deacon's home (informal question & answer time for the deacons and the candidate)

Sunday
- Breakfast: Candidate/wife on their own
- 8:45 A.M. Preach early and late morning services

- Lunch: With the assistant pastor and his wife
- Congregational question-and-answer time (3:30-4:45 P.M.) in the main auditorium
- 6:00 P.M. Preach the evening service
- 7:15 P.M. Congregational social in the church fellowship hall to informally meet with the candidate and his wife
- Dinner: With the youth pastor if the candidate wishes

Monday
- Breakfast: Candidate/wife on their own
- 8:30 A.M. Candidate meets with the school staff for prayer
- 9:30 A.M. Candidate preaches to the high school student body in chapel
- 10:00 A.M. Candidate meets with the school administrator
- 11:30 A.M. Lunch with the entire pastoral staff and their wives
- 1:00 P.M. Candidate meets with assistant pastor
- Candidate meets with the church secretaries (all at once) informally
- 3:00 P.M. "Meet the Candidate" time for all school staff (in the school library)
- 4:00 P.M. Meet with assistant pastor if needed
- Dinner: Candidate/deacon chairman and wives

Tuesday
- 9:05 A.M. Fly out of International Airport

Wednesday
- 7:00 P.M. Special business meeting called for congregational question-and-answer time (moderated by an assistant pastor) and the vote to call the candidate to be our pastor (conducted by the deacon chairman)
- Immediately after the evening service there will be a voluntary deacons' meeting in the senior pastor's office. We'll be contacting the candidate on the speakerphone with the results of the vote.

APPENDIX K

Your Church Pastoral Contract

Compensation Package for Pastor _____ _____
Date

This document is to be reviewed annually by the deacons and/or their representatives (prior to the approval of the Annual Church Budget).

Basic Salary: $ _____

TSA: _____ % of the base salary

Housing: To be chosen by the pastor with a "tax sheltered" option available

Library Allowance: Will be reimbursed up to $ _____ per year for the purchase of personal materials that will assist in his study.

Car Allowance: 100% paid for by the church. The vehicle is for official business of the church. The pastor will use discretion during daily and weekly use. Valued use of vehicle approx. $ _____ per year. A gas card is available for church-related business. Vehicle maintenance and insurance shall be paid for by the church.

Health Insurance: Workmen's Compensation
$ _____ life
Dental/Optical/Medical as per current church plan

Disability Insurance: Present policy starts after 30 days continuous leave.

Vacation: _____ weeks paid by church per year (not more than _____ Sundays can be missed)
_____ weeks will be allowed after _____ years of service (not more than _____ Sundays can be missed)

Business Days: _____ business days will be provided per year. These business days are to be used for church-related business that takes the pastor away from his normal business hours within the church.

Not more than _____ Sundays per year should be missed using business days. Scheduling should be done allowing one pastoral staff member to be on the church grounds Monday through Friday (if at all possible).

The pastor's calendar will be reviewed monthly with the chairman of the deacons. Should there be a need to request business days in excess of the _____ days provided, approval will be at the discretion of the chairman of the deacons and a report of the overage will be made by the pastor (or deacon chairman) at the next regularly scheduled deacons' meeting.

Work Week: Defined as a minimum of five days/week in which time is spent keeping regular office hours—to be determined by the pastor (but communicated to the deacons).

Office Equipment: A cell phone and/or pager will be available to the pastor for church-related business. Itemized billings will be reviewed by the deacon chairman and/or vice chairman. All equipment remains the property of the church unless purchased by the pastor with personal funds.

Miscellaneous: Christmas and New Year's are a family time, thus only minimal time should be spent in the office. The pastor is to use discretion in allowing maximum time off. Church offices are closed on all major holidays.

Educational Expenses: Will be borne by the church with the prior approval of the deacons.

Moving Expenses: Will be borne by the church with the prior approval of the deacon chairman and vice chairman.

_____   _____
Deacon Chairman   Pastor

_____   _____
Deacon Vice Chairman   Treasurer

APPENDIX L

Search Committee Procedural Suggestions

General Thoughts

- Deacon chairman will keep tabs on and monitor the progress of the search committee and keep the deacon board informed.

- Search committee chairman will keep the church body informed of progress at least on a monthly basis.

- Go slow! God pays dividends for patience.

- Dr. Harry Love: Wait three months before having a person in the pulpit that could be considered a candidate. The only possible exception would be if the assistant pastor is considering the position (then go even longer).

- Dr. VanGelderen: Pursue only one man until either the man or the church accepts or rejects the proposal.

- It is not the purpose of the search committee to call a man. The search committee represents the church and will leave the final decision to the congregation.

Procedures for acquiring a new pastor

- Upon the vacating of the pulpit by the senior pastor, the deacons will appoint an interim pastor. If there is advance knowledge of the pulpit being vacated, the deacons may choose to make their appointment prior to the vacancy.

- The deacons (no full-time staff) comprise the search committee.

- Establish committee goals. These should include but are not limited to

  1. Setting aside a time for regularly called meetings

  2. Study of God's Word (both individually and corporately)

  3. Having times of prayer and fasting

  4. Laying aside our own personal aspirations and seeking those of God

  5. Working resolutely but not hastily

- Establish a "Candidate Pool" (even if the assistant pastor candidates)

  1. Contact men that know your church and its philosophy. These may include evangelists, missionaries, pastors, college professors, and administrators.

  2. Be open to your own membership's recommendations.

  3. Be careful of any recommendation from anyone not having been in your church or of the unsolicited résumé.

- Establish a Candidate Questionnaire, or Profile

- Professional protocol may demand that the assistant pastor get consideration first.

  1. You proceed until either the assistant pastor accepts or rejects the position or the congregation accepts or rejects him.

  2. If the assistant pastor doesn't want to candidate, he must go public in order not to cause problems in the church.

- Contact each potential candidate personally prior to sending out the questionnaire. You may choose to include a statement mentioning that several men have recommended his name for consideration and you want to know if he (the man being contacted) is "approachable."

- Having all returned questionnaires in hand, narrow the list to three men. Sermon tapes may be requested at this point. Through prayer and godly counsel, narrow that list further to the point that the committee agrees on the premier candidate. Pursue that man until God closes all doors.

- Check most, if not all, references. Seek additional reference information from contacts that know the applicant but have not been suggested by the applicant. Establish a list of questions that will be asked of each reference in order to insure comparative analysis.

- Visit that man's church. Look at every aspect of the service including the spirit of the people. At this point the potential candidate may wish to visit your church for the same purpose of evaluation. Share with the potential candidate a current version of the church profile.

- Search Committee Interview:
  Ask for a list of every special speaker, missionary (and his board), and evangelist he's had in his church over the past two years. Also bring to the interview a music schedule for the same period of time. Ask to check the potential candidate's credit rating. NOTE: Have less inter-

est in a man's total indebtedness than whether he pays his bills on time.

- The search committee should present to the deacons, for their approval, a contract that will be offered to the candidate should he accept the call to be your senior pastor.

  1. Search Committee: Some of the committee have heard the candidate preach in person, but all members will meet him at the interview level.

  2. Deacons: A meeting (afternoon and/or evening) will be set up for the deacons to question the candidate.

  3. Church and/or school staff can meet with the candidate.

  4. The laymen question-and-answer time on the afternoon of the candidacy may be moderated by the deacon chairman, search committee chairman, or candidate.

- Candidate Sunday

  1. A personal profile of the candidate should be included in the bulletin.

  2. In Sunday school, notice is given asking for written questions from the laymen and is given to the search committee chairman or the deacon chairman. He will compile the questions. NOTE: The candidate has the option of fielding the questions impromptu.

  3. Candidate preaches Sunday morning service.

  4. Question-and-answer session for any member wishing to attend.

  5. Candidate preaches Sunday night.

- Vote on the candidate at the next Wednesday night service. Either you have a pastor or you don't. If the candidate is rejected, return to your candidate pool that will now contain two men and proceed from there, following the same procedure as before. When the new senior pastor has signed the contract with the church, all potential candidates' personally identifiable information collected during the pastoral search should be destroyed.

- Communicate with others the news of the congregation's call extended to your new pastor and his acceptance of that call. Make sure you communicate with any of the men you were still considering in the candidate pool as well as anyone who was instrumental in giving you guidance.

APPENDIX M

Business Expense Sheet

Name		Event		Date(s)				

Date	Business Purpose	Mileage	Gas	Breakfast	Lunch	Dinner	Lodging	Misc
	Totals							

Signature		Date		Grand Total